UP!

DISCARD

AND FOR MY NEXT TRIC I WILL ATTEMPT TO BREATH UNDE WATER.

...tunity to look at your
...er it is not appropriate

...he gallery and hope that

RANDOM HOUSE

BERTELSMANN

Other People's Rejection Letters

Relationship Enders, Career Killers,
and 150 Other Letters You'll Be Glad
You Didn't Receive

Edited by Bill Shapiro

Clarkson Potter/Publishers
New York

1745 BROADWAY, NEW YORK, NY 10019 · TELEPHONE 212 782-9000

REJECTED

April 15

For more letters, visit
otherpeoplesrejectionletters.com

Copyright © 2010 by Bill Shapiro

Published in the United States by Clarkson Potter/
Publishers, an imprint of the Crown Publishing Group,
a division of Random House, Inc., New York.
www.crownpublishing.com
www.clarksonpotter.com

CLARKSON POTTER is a trademark and POTTER with colophon
is a registered trademark of Random House, Inc.

Library of Congress Cataloging-in-Publication Data

Shapiro, Bill.
   Other people's rejection letters/Bill Shapiro.—1st ed.
      p. cm.
   1. Rejection (Psychology)—Humor. I. Title.
   PN6231.R39S53 2010
   816.008'0353—dc22
                                                2009028658

ISBN 978-0-307-45964-0

Printed in China

Design by Amy Sly
Illustrations on pp. 6-9 by Jim Massey

10 9 8 7 6 5 4 3 2 1

First Edition

Not this place

INTRODUCTION

In 1956, the Museum of Modern Art shrugged off Andy Warhol's gift of a drawing, citing their "severely limited gallery and storage space."

In 1962, Jimi Hendrix, then a private in the U.S. Army, was slammed by his superior officer in a report for, among other things, not being able to "carry on an intelligent conversation."

In 1938, F. Scott Fitzgerald sent a caustic rant to his daughter that included this little gem: "What you have done to please me or make me proud is practically negligible."

In 1976, a skinny girl named Dani with hair the color of cinnamon left a note on my summer-camp bunk bed that read, in its entirety, "Billy: I like Jason."

You'll find all of the above rejection letters in this book—except the one from Dani. Part of me wishes I had held on to that note; part of me can't believe how pathetic it is that I remember it thirty-four years on. But I do remember it—torn notebook paper, loopy red ink— and even today it is not hard to summon its sting.

I suspect that upon reading her note, I hated Jason quite a bit, and probably Dani, too. I am confident, though, that I hated myself more. (That's one thing that has always interested me about rejection: whom you blame for it. Whom do you hold responsible when you don't get the cute girl with cinnamon hair or the good job or the platinum card?) Over the years, the memory of Dani's note has floated back to me from time to time, and when it does, I find myself wondering what effect her four-word rejection had on me. Did it encourage me to step up my game when faced with future competitors? Or did it make me fearful of further rejection? A rejection letter, after all, has remarkable power: A single piece of paper with a dozen words—even a form

letter typed years earlier by an inexperienced, possibly hungover assistant—can sway or scar a life, causing one person to give up his dreams, another to work harder to achieve them.

Lately, I've been thinking about rejection quite a bit. Who hasn't? In fact, it's safe to say that over the last two years, more rejection letters have been written in this country than at any time in its 234-year history—rejections for mortgages and small-business loans, eviction and foreclosure notices, for grant money and credit cards and college scholarships. And everybody knows somebody who's received a "due to the current economic conditions, we have made the difficult decision to downsize our staff" note . . . followed, some weeks later, by letters that start like this: "Unfortunately, due to the number of applications for this position . . ." With that in mind, I began collecting other people's rejection letters. I had gathered love letters for a previous book and, given the times, rejection letters seemed a natural topic to explore: a not-exactly-rose-colored window into the national zeitgeist.

But here's what I discovered: Reading other people's rejection letters didn't tell me half as much about the spirit of the times as it told me about myself. Sitting at my desk, surrounded by leaning towers of rejection, I must have looked at more than seven hundred letters, notes, text messages, and e-mails. As I flipped through those first few, I felt comforted, although not in the way I expected. There was no swell of schadenfreude, no dark joy at the misfortune of others, no desire to say "nah-nah-nah-nah-nah." In fact, I saw that no one is alone in getting shot down in love and work and creative pursuits—not the pilot sent packing fifteen times from NASA's astronaut program (he kept trying!) or the would-be novelist who mailed me most of the sixty-four "sorry, it's not for us" notes her manuscript had earned her. I saw all these people taking beautiful chances with their lives.

Which led me to look at my own. Where were my rejection letters? Where was the evidence that, win or lose, I had put myself on the line? I thought about all the opportunities I could have chased and, while I've certainly grabbed a few brass rings over the years, I couldn't help but wonder if they were the ones always safely in reach. Did I calibrate my chances just right? Did I self-select for success? What would my life be like now if, instead of reaching . . . I had jumped? Those questions now stared me full in the face. As it turns out, I'm not the only one to have those feelings; they're echoed in a painfully honest letter toward the end of this book.

Call it a case of "ask and ye shall receive." Or maybe just call it irony. About two days after I wrote the paragraph just above and vowed to take more chances and risk more rejection, I had dinner with a woman I'll call Johanna, a woman I was falling for. I'd known her a while and we'd gone out a few times in a sort of undefined way— was it a date . . . or was it just dinner? Walking down the street after two hours of amazing dinner conversation, I realized that my moment had come. I breathed deep and put an end to the ambiguity: I asked her out on a date-date. She quietly said yes, but the (lovely) e-mail I received the next morning included the following line: "I have enjoyed our, uh, 'outings' together and would like to do it again. But I don't think I want to take it down a dating road."

What separates a rejection letter from a spoken rejection is that you can reread it. And this I did many times with Johanna's note. I was caught off guard—I thought she felt what I felt—so I went through her words carefully to make sure I hadn't misread anything. I had not. I felt terrible, alone in the world and very small. I tried to bolster myself with homilies along the lines of "Well, at least you took the risk," but they stuck in my throat and died there.

An hour later, I turned back to her e-mail looking for clues as to why she'd cut me loose and, to be honest, for any possible openings she may have left me. (Not many.) I then copied Johanna's e-mail to my hard drive. Why do that? Her message was clear, the case closed. On reflection, I suppose I kept it for two reasons: to beat myself up, to confirm that my deepest suspicions about myself were true. But I also saved it as a sort of time capsule, with the intent that, one day, I would look back on the note and say to myself (and, silently, to Johanna), "See. I didn't need you. Things turned out OK after all."

At that point, perhaps, I will drag her rejection letter to the trash.

EVERYONE ASKS: SO HOW DID YOU GET THESE LETTERS?

I hit up my friends and then friends of friends, and then I enlisted a team of clever reporters from across the country to help with the hunt. (These notes are hard to come by; rejection letters are not typically the stuff of scrapbooks.) Some letters have been slightly altered to protect the writer's identity or that of the recipient, and not all letters are printed in their entirety. Finally, here's the part where I mention the book's website (www.otherpeoplesrejectionletters.com), so if you're looking for more rejection, now you know exactly where to find it. May I leave you with one final thought? If you've received a rejection letter, count yourself as lucky, because the alternative—silence—is a hundred times worse.

Kevin, I said

no. —Meghan

WALT DISNEY'S Snow White and the Seven Dwarfs

June 7, 1938

Miss Mary V. Ford
Searcy,
Arkansas

Dear Miss Ford:

Your letter of recent date has been received in the Inking and Painting Department for reply.

Women do not do any of the creative work in connection with preparing the cartoons for the screen, as that work is performed entirely by young men. For this reason girls are not considered for the training school.

The only work open to women consists of tracing the characters on clear celluloid sheets with India ink and filling in the tracings on the reverse side with paint according to directions.

In order to apply for a position as "Inker" or "Painter" it is necessary that one appear at the Studio, bringing samples of pen and ink and water color work. It would not be advisable to come to Hollywood with the above specifically in view, as there are really very few openings in comparison with the number of girls who apply.

Yours very truly,

WALT DISNEY PRODUCTIONS, LTD.

By: *Mary Cleave*

MEC

WALT DISNEY PRODUCTIONS, Ltd.
2719 HYPERION · HOLLYWOOD, CAL.

Rock,
I have a policy of not giving away locks of my hair.
Sorry,

Thank you for submitting. Unfortunately, the work you sent us is quite terrible. Please forgive the form rejection, but it would take too much of my time to tell you exactly how terrible it was. So again, sorry for the form letter.

NEW DELTA REVIEW

Department of English
15 Allen Hall
Louisiana State University
Baton Rouge, LA 70803-5001
www.lsu.edu/newdeltareview
new-delta@lsu.edu

HEADQUARTERS · UNITED STATES MARINE CORPS · WASHINGTON, D.C. 20380
The Few. The Proud. The Marines.

Mr. Bill Dobrow
148 Poineer Dr
West Hartford, CT 06117

Dear Mr. Dobrow:

We appreciate your interest in the Marine Corps.

However, since you are twelve, you won't be eligible to be
a Marine for a while. But as our way of showing appreciation
for your interest, we are enclosing a special Marine memento.

I want to give you this advice: The Marine Corps wants you to
stay in school and get your diploma. The more education you
have, the more valuable you will be -- to yourself, and to the
Marines. Then, when you have graduated, ask one of our re-
cruiters about the variety of technical training skills we
offer.

Thanks again for your interest in the Corps.

                              Sincerely,

                              Dave Turner

                              Dave Turner
                              Major, U. S. Marine Corps

DT:und
Enc.: Eagle Iron-On

Dear Gran
I got y
I can't co
have othe
I love yo

dma,
our letter. But
me because I hav
r plans.
u.

Love,
Naomi

SCHOOL OF
MEDICINE

YORK UNIVERSITY

PO BOX ▮▮▮▮▮
HARTFORD CT 06150

RETURN SERVICE REQUESTED

000297 1 AT 0.346

APT ▮

▮▮▮ ATLANTIC AVENUE
BROOKLYN NY   11216

1000297

Return to sender

Recipient kicked out shortly after having online sex with the sender. Recipient now lives with his parents in the suburbs. Sender can use her formidable internet skills to find the forwarding address.

THE WHITE HOUSE
WASHINGTON

Dear Friend:

Thank you for contacting the White
House Greetings Office.

The President honors citizens with
appropriate cards only on their 80th or
subsequent birthdays and 50th or subsequent
wedding anniversaries. Because your
request does not meet these longstanding
White House guidelines, we regret that we
will not be able to honor it at this time.

We appreciate your thoughtfulness and
hope that we will be able to assist you
sometime in the near future.

On behalf of President Clinton, thank
you for your interest in his Administration.

Sincerely,

Jamie Shell Williams

Jamie Shell Williams
Director
Office of Presidential Inquiries

March 4, 2004

Dear Penny,
   I've been thinking about our conversation at your last appointment and feel I should apologize for my defensiveness at your comments about your hair. I have felt for a while that you're not happy with your hair. Your last appointment confirmed that. There comes a time when a stylist/client relationship has run its course and would be best for both of us to not continue. I feel you should find another stylist who might better understand your needs. I will be canceling your future appointments.

Sincerely,

Annie

CIGNA HealthCare

May 5, 2006

ROSLYN ~~████~~
████ WHITE SANDS LANE
DAVIS CA 9561█

Re:
Participant ID #: U22947████
Reference Code: BS0CMZK1
Intracorp*, on behalf of Your Employer Plan

Dear ROSLYN ~~████~~

We received a coverage request on 09/01/2006 for you for the following service(s):

• Reduction of large breast (19318)

Based on your eligibility and health care benefit plan's provisions, limitations and exclusions, we have determined the requested services are not covered. This decision was based on the following:

(19318)
Reduction of large breast is not covered under your plan

Decisions about your medical care are yours to make along with your treating provider. We want you to make an informed decision, so please discuss your treatment options with your provider. If you choose to proceed with the requested service(s), any claims associated with the denied request will not be considered for payment. Please refer to your benefit plan documents to get additional details about your benefit plan coverage.

If you or your provider would like to obtain copies (free of charge) of the documents, records or other information relied upon to make this decision, please call the Health Services Department at 800.244.6224.

And did
you give
a shit?

Back to Messages   Mark as Unread   Report Spam   Delete   ▲ ▼

Hi

Between You and ___

Lauren ___ September 25 at 12:25pm

so you have the courage to say something on facebook but not in person...cool. There is this thing called knocking, you should try it sometime. I'll tell ashley you said hello. take care.

September 25 at 12:25pm

REDACTED

Lauren ___ September 25 at 12:26pm

oh please, you're an adult ___ act like one. Don't try to guilt me into feeling bad for you...on facebook no less. If you felt like you needed to tell me to have a good trip then just say it. But really I find it hard to believe you felt so compelled to say anything considering you stopped talking to me about 2 months ago, but that's a whole different discussion which we don't need to get into.

Look, I'm not mad at you (and i haven't been) and i don't hold anything against you so you don't act like I'm making your life so difficult by having my door shut, at my house, while i was changing clothes....really I feel sooooo bad why would I do a thing like that...

REDACTED — September 25 at 12:26pm

Lauren ▬ September 25 at 9:27am

blahhhh blaahhhh blahhhh bitter much? are you seriously doing this right now? You're seriously going to act like you've always been a good person, always had "our" best interest at heart, always been a good friend to me? Get real. Yes I slowed down the pace we were going at and I'll accept blame for that...but for good reason, I mean, look, you bailed after a couple of unreturned phone calls. Not that I was surprised or anything, it's kind of your m.o. ANYWAYS, like I said, unlike you who seems to have all sorts of hostility about the situation, I have never been angry with you. I was the one who extended an invitation to get together over thanksgiving, but once again it wasn't convenient for you. Seriously ▬, I really hope that one day you can look back with more perspective than you have now and see things for the way they truly are. I also hope one day we can be friends without all this other bullshit in the way, and I was ready to do that but clearly you are not. But like you said we have different lives and honestly right now, I'm so thankful for that. Take care, please don't write me back. If you really need to say something to me then be a man, and do it in person.

Back to Messages

If you send ▬ a message, you will give him permission to view your list of friends, as well as your Basic, Work and Education info for one month.

April 27, 2009

RE: Notice Pursuant to the Federal and New York State
       Worker Adjustment and Retraining Notification Act

Dear

We are providing this notice to satisfy the requirements of the Federal Worker Adjustment and Retraining Notification Act of 1988, and the New York State Worker Adjustment and Retraining Notification Act, laws which require advance written notice of certain layoffs and closings.

Condé Nast Portfolio, located at 4 Times Square, New York, New York 10036, will be permanently ceasing publication and closing its entire operations. The closing will be on April 27, 2009. You will not be required to report to work after that date. You will, however, remain on payroll, with full benefits and pay until ⬛⬛⬛ unless you obtain employment within the Company or elsewhere.

You do not have the right to replace another employee instead of separating from employment with Condé Nast Portfolio (i.e., no bumping rights).

You are also

Very truly yours,

Mary Macnab Kennedy
Group Executive Director

oct. 17

We have been through this again and again: you say
you want to see me. I tell you thaxt it won't wxrkx
work, that it never does. We talk about it. I agree to
come over to tlak about it more. We force smiles, small
txax talk. And then you say something that hurts me and
Icall you on it, and then you say I'm being too sensitive,
that I was always too sensitive. xxxxxxxxxxxxxxx Or maybe
I say something sarcastic becausex I don't want to get hurt xx
again, and then you get upset. Then it escalates and we end
up screaming at each otherx and pounding on tables. Neither
of us backs down. ever. Then you tell me what a shitty son
i am. I tell you that I hate yourx guts and don't need you
in my life. I walk out the door.

I do not want xto keep doing this, Mom. I can't. It's too
painful and it's not getting better. So I am going to be
out of touch. I will not return your calls so don't bother.
I will call you in six months. We need xx to break this
cycle one way or the other.

Bethesda, MD
20816

September 1, 1998

Dear ▓▓▓▓

▓▓▓▓▓▓▓ requested that I write a critique for you. Thank you for your patience, as I know that you requested this some time ago.

Let me preface this critique by saying that the use of very specific characters with names and developed "personalities" don't work well overall if the audience is not previously aware of them. Characters like Snoopy, Garfield and the like work because the audience has had exposure to them via cartoons and television. In addition, we do not advertise, nor do we have control over the physical placement of cards in the racks (they could not be placed together to make a strong presentation). This makes that much more difficult for cards of this nature to do well.

I would say that overall, the images are cute, but sometimes the image and the copy just don't mesh, as in the case of the "puppy love" anniversary card. I don't know what sequence you work in, but most of our artists tend to develop the copy and determine what they want to say before the actual image is created. I think that you'll find this to be the easiest way to create.

Some specifics:
-the images tend to look not to look like dogs, as they tend to have human expressions and bodies.
-the "on the mend" card has a big reach between the image and copy, perhaps this would be better as a Mother's Day card with revised copy.

I hope you find this information helpful. We wish you luck in your artistic endeavors.

Kind Regards,

Gretchen Hoffman

Gretchen Hoffman
New Artist Coordinator

C. WILLIAM EDWARDS
Director of Admission
321 Pyne Administration Bldg.
Princeton, New Jersey

BERNARD S. ADAMS
Assistant Director
JOSEPH L. BOLSTER, JR.
Assistant Director

February 11, 1957

Dear Mr. Wax:

In reply to your recent letter, I
regret that we must inform you that
Princeton University has no Law
School.

Sincerely yours,

Joseph L. Bolster, Jr.

Mr. Harvey Wax
1805 Washtenaw
Ann Arbor, Michigan

es

I wish that I just go with scenario. I be quite fun. able to have with you that casual sex. style.

could easily
this
bet it could
But I am not
a friendship
includes
It's not my

April 26, 1993

Arthur Gonzalez
3038 Texas Street
Oakland, CA 94602

Dear Mr. Gonzalez:

Thank you for sending me the enclosed materials on your work, which I enjoyed seeing. Unfortunately, I am unable to help you. I do, however, want to wish you continued success with your career and to thank you for your interest in the Max Protetch Gallery.

Sincerely,

Jeffrey Hoffeld
Director

Encl.
JH:de

ARTIST

ARTIST

It will never be.

GALLERY

The
Louis
Comfort
Tiffany
Foundation

5 December 1987

It is my sad duty to inform you that you have not been chosen for
a Tiffany Foundation award. The Jury, composed of Frances Barth,
Robert Blackburn, Thomas Buechner, Roy Lichtenstein, Ned Rifkin,
Paul Smith and Roberta Smith, seriously considered your work, but
unfortunately was able to recommend only 20 artists from the pool
of approximately 260 to the Board of Trustees for grants in
painting, sculpture and crafts this year. I wish the Foundation
could award as many grants as there are talented candidates.

Thank you for contributing to the high and serious level of this
year's competition.

Unfortunately, I am unable to return your slides as you neglected
to send a self-addressed stamped envelope. If you wish, I will
forward them to you on receipt of appropriate postage, in this
case $1.50. Or, should you be in the New York area, you can pick
them up at Sperone Westwater, 142 Greene Street, Tuesday -
Saturday, 10 - 6. Please call ahead on the Foundation line.

I am sorry for this inconvenience.

Sincerely,

Angela Westwater
President
AW/jm

SAD DOODY.

NED   Roberta   Roy

Rereading over this note, I find aspects of it that trouble me, and rather than let them wait, on the chance they might grow bigger, I thought perhaps I should address them now, with the hope that we can, at the least, agree to disagree and move on.

First off, you're not my Jewish aunt -- I already have one, thank you -- and it's not for you to tell me that I need to be a good Jew. I assume you meant that somewhat light-heartedly, but I find it a little offensive -- as you might if, for example, I exhorted you, in whatever tone of voice, to be a good mother. My relationship to my own religion is my own business, and needs no correcting by an outsider.

Secondly, I find the whole tone of this somewhat patronizing, lecturing, the more since I have repeatedly told you that there's nothing I can do, nothing I should do, and nothing I intend to do, about this situation. For the record, my reasons aren't that it falls to me to honor someone else's wedding vows: how they interpret those vows is up to them, as individuals and as a couple. It's none of my business, and in any case, no interloper can wreck a marriage that isn't already wrecked, and no man of restraint can save a marriage that isn't already strong.

Nevertheless, as I say and have said, I don't intend to do anything, just because (a) it seems preposterously unlikely that any advance on my part would be anything but unwelcome, and (b) because even if it was welcome, it would probably be wildly destructive, not least of all to myself.

-- But I don't think I need you tell me how to be a 'stand-up guy'; I don't need moral instruction, and if you felt like I was behaving in an unseemly manner, I would hope you could tell me so without talking to me as if I was a small, wayward child. As I said to you the other night, I've done absolutely nothing improper, said nothing improper.

Thirdly, I think you ought to acknowledge that the only thing remotely like encouragement I have received from any quarter, to pursue this, is from you -- both in your original email suggesting that my flirting that night wasn't entirely unilateral, and then in your description of her reaction when you gave her my book.

That's OK, really -- intrigue is fun, matchmaking, even as a fantasy, is fun. But it strikes me as a little disingenuous for you to then turn around and lecture me about morals, and the need for me to back off. I haven't done anything that I might need to back off from.

What worries me is that a situation has been set up in which everyone gets to whisper and intrigue and have some fun, but if it all goes wrong, it's suddenly all my fault. I want to avoid that.

As for friendship, as I've already explained to you, that may -- or may not -- be somewhat more difficult for me. As things stand, I'm the one who goes home alone every night, and if I decide that I don't need an especially painful reminder of that right now, that'll be my decision, and my choice.

OK?

Hello ⬛,

We've found out about your plans with the surgery, but moreover the manner in which you have chosen to carry out the process as well as your overall conduct in regards to the events of the wedding. ⬛ and I are both very shocked and hurt about how you have chosen to treat us. You are no longer welcome to be a bridesmaid at our wedding. Do not treat us in such a poor manner during our wedding again. We will send you a check in the mail for the amount of your bridesmaid dress and we wish you the best of luck with your surgery and weight loss.

Sincerely,

⬛ and ⬛

THE MUSEUM OF MODERN ART

NEW YORK 19

11 WEST 53rd STREET
TELEPHONE: CIRCLE 5-8900
CABLES: MODERNART, NEW-YORK

THE MUSEUM COLLECTIONS

October 18, 1956

Dear Mr. Warhol:

Last week our Committee on the Museum Collections held its first meeting of the fall season and had a chance to study your drawing entitled <u>Shoe</u> which you so generously offered as a gift to the Museum.

I regret that I must report to you that the Committee decided, after careful consideration, that they ought not to accept it for our Collection.

Let me explain that because of our severely limited gallery and storage space we must turn down many gifts offered, since we feel it is not fair to accept as a gift a work which may be shown only infrequently.

Nevertheless, the Committee has asked me to pass on to you their thanks for your generous expression of interest in our Collection.

Sincerely,

Alfred H. Barr, Jr.
Director of the Museum Collections

Mr. Andy Warhol
242 Lexington Avenue
New York, New York

AHB:bj

P.S. The drawing may be picked up from the Museum at your
     convenience.

Recording Requested By
When Recorded Mail To

Cal-Western Reconveyance Corp.
P.O. Box 22004
525 East Main Street
El Cajon CA 92022-9004

Recording Requested By
Service Link

Trustee Sale No. 11487█ ██

Loan No. XXXXXX2417 Ref: ████████ ████

Space Above This Line For Recorder's Use

NOTICE OF DEFAULT

IMPORTANT NOTICE

IF YOUR PROPERTY IS IN FORECLOSURE BECAUSE YOU ARE BEHIND IN YOUR PAYMENTS, IT MAY BE SOLD WITHOUT ANY COURT ACTION, and you may have legal right to bring your account in good standing by paying all of your past due payments plus permitted costs and expenses within the time permitted by law for reinstatement of your account, which is normally five business days prior to the date set for the sale of your property. No sale date may be set until three months from the date this notice of default may be recorded (which date of recordation appears on this notice). This amount is $9,124.00 as of May 27, 2008, and will increase until your account becomes current. While your property is in foreclosure, you still must pay other obligations (such as insurance and taxes) required by your note and deed of trust or mortgage. If you fail to make future payments on the loan, pay taxes on the property, provide insurance on the property, or pay other obligations as required in the note and deed of trust or mortgage, the beneficiary or mortgagee may insist that you do so in order to reinstate your account in good standing. In addition, the beneficiary or mortgagee may require as a condition to reinstatement that you provide reliable written evidence that you paid all senior liens, property taxes, and hazard insurance premiums.

Upon your written request, the beneficiary or mortgagee will give you a written itemization of the entire amount you must pay. You may not have to pay the entire unpaid portion of your account, even though full payment was demanded, but you must pay all amounts in default at the time payment is made. However, you and your beneficiary or mortgagee may mutually agree in writing prior to the time the notice of sale is posted (which may not be earlier than the end of the three-month period stated above) to, among other things, (1) provide additional time in which to cure the default by transfer of the property or otherwise; or (2) establish a schedule of payments in order to cure your default; or both (1) and (2).

Following the expiration of the time period referred to in the first paragraph of this notice, unless the obligation being foreclosed upon or a separate written agreement between you and your creditor permits a longer period, you have only the legal right to stop the sale of your property by paying the entire amount demanded by your creditor.

To find out the amount you must pay, or to arrange for payment to stop the foreclosure, or if your property is in foreclosure for any other reason, contact:
AURORA LOAN SERVICES LLC

C/O Cal-Western Reconveyance Corporation
P.O. Box 22004
525 East Main Street
El Cajon CA 92022-9004
(619)590-9200

If you have any questions, you should contact a lawyer or the governmental agency which may have insured your loan.

Page 1 of 2

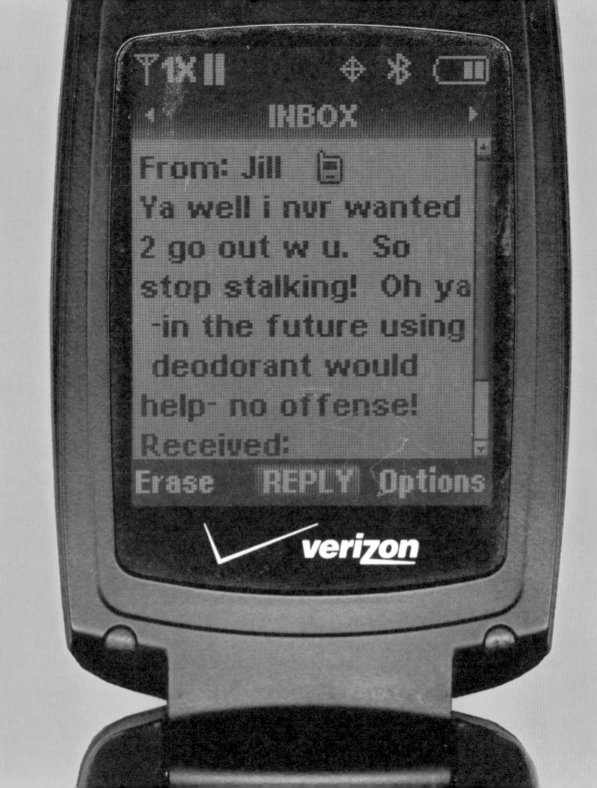

March 24, 1989

Mr. Thomas P. Stinson
2111 Kasold Drive #102D
Lawrence, Kansas 66044

Dear Mr. Stinson:

Your clips have now been evaluated along with those of
many other applicants. I'm sorry to say that the
editors who reviewed your work concluded that, while
your clips showed talent and energy, other candidates
have skills that are more fully developed.

I hope this is not too disappointing. Your interest in
The Times is geatly appreciated.

Sincerely,

Marie Davitt

Marie Davitt
Manager
Clerical News Staff

DNA
DIAGNOSTICS
CENTER

DNA Parentage
Test Report

Report Date   4/10/2004

Case 207764	CHILD		Alleged FATHER	
Name	▬▬▬▬▬		▬▬▬▬▬	
Race			Caucasian	
Date Collected	4-2-04		4-2-04	
Test No.	207764-20		207764-30	

Locus	PI	Allele Sizes		Allele Sizes	
D8S1179	0.00	15	16	11	13
D21S11	0.00	28		29	31.2
D7S820	0.00	10		8	11
CSF1PO	1.56	12		12	13
D3S1358	1.68	15	18	14	18
THO1	0.82	9	9.3	8	9.3
D13S317	1.78	11	12	12	
D16S539	0.00	9	12	11	
D2S1338	1.16	16	17	17	26
D19S433	1.37	14.2	15	13	15
VWA	1.19	15	16	14	16
TPOX	1.86	8		8	
D18S51	0.00	13	14	16	17
D5S818	0.00	11	12	9	13
FGA	3.16	22	24	22	24

Interpretation   Combined Paternity Index **0**   Probability of Paternity **0%**

The alleged father is excluded as the biological father of the child named above. This conclusion
is based on the non-matching alleles observed at the loci listed above with a PI equal to zero. The
alleged father lacks the genetic markers that must be contributed to the child by the biological
father. The probability of paternity is 0%.

Subscribed and sworn before me on April 10, 2004

Edward Harris,
Notary Public, State of Ohio
My Commission Expires July 24, 2008

I, the undersigned, verify that the interpretation of the
results is correct as reported, and the testing procedure
was conducted in accordance with the AABB guidelines.

Thomas M. Reid, Ph.D.
Assistant Laboratory Director

205 CORPORATE COURT   FAIRFIELD   OHIO   45014   PHONE: 513.881.7800   FAX: 513.881.7803

You are very
Stubborn but.
you are Mine

Some time I think
your are a big jack ass
but I love you
                mommie

Dear ⬛⬛⬛⬛,

I didn't mean to take so long to respond to you. I've been sort of overloaded, and also it's not easy to know exactly what to say or how to say it. Or maybe it's just difficult to tell you that your being in my life brings me frustration and pain that I don't want to feel and to tell you that you have to stop calling and emailing me. Each time I get a message or an email from you it upsets me. It reminds me of how far your perception of our relationship is from reality and how much it is and always has been about what you feel like having in the moment, how little you consider or are even aware of me. You leave me messages as if we're suddenly friends – or worse, as if we're involved – and as if we've been communicating all along. The reality is that I know almost nothing about what goes on in your life and you know even less about mine. It just makes me feel bad when you expect me to laugh with you about things that came between us, like ⬛⬛⬛⬛ taking the job you could have had at Cornell, your missing therapy, or whatever – the many things you seem to think I'll find cute and funny when really they just remind me of your empty promises, your lack of consideration, the pain you've caused me, and your obliviousness to all of it.

At this point we really have no relationship other than what's in your head. The me that you say you think about or have conversations with is not me, and your references to your thoughts about me just make me realize how much all along the relationship you believed we were having was about what was going on in your head and had little to do with any interaction with me as an actual person. You have a right to whatever thoughts you have, but your thoughts about me don't give you the right to disrupt my life – and they certainly don't give you the right to leave messages about what I should be doing with my life; the decisions I make – for instance, about whether to have children – are personal and it has been a long time since you had any right to weigh in on them.

I don't like to have to be so harsh, but it seems like the only way to get through to you. No feelings I have for you and no connection we share makes it worth the pain and disappointment that involvement with you has always brought, and when I acknowledge the positive things that exist between us you hear only that and focus on it as if that means yes, as if that love or connection is enough to outweigh the many negatives, when in fact time and experience with you have taught me that the opposite is true.

None of this is easy to say, and it's even harder to feel it – both to have gone through it so many times and to now have it stirred up yet again. So what I'm saying is stop calling and emailing me; let this go and let me go on with my life.

From: info@enews.staplescenter.com
To: @hotmail.com
Subject: The Michael Jackson Public Memorial Service at STAPLES Center
Date: Mon, 6 Jul 2009 02:11:41 -0400

Sorry, we regret to inform you that your registration was not selected.
If you are using a mobile device or can't see the images, click here.

Thank you for your registration.

Sorry, we regret to inform you that your
registration to attend the Public Memorial
Service for Michael Jackson was not selected.

Hundreds of thousands registered, but only a few
can be in attendance.

Do Not Reply to this email. This is an unattended email box and your inquiry will not be answered.

© 2009 STAPLES Center. All Rights Reserved.
STAPLES Center • 1111 S. Figueroa Street • Los Angeles , CA 90015

If you can't see the images in this email, click here.

You received this email because you subscribed at staplescenter.com for the Michael Jackson Public Memorial Service.
Visit staplescenter.com for more information.

AEG STAPLES Center is owned and operated by a subsidiary of AEG.

Privacy Policy | Unsubscribe

FROM ARTHUR C. FIFIELD, PUBLISHER,
13, CLIFFORD'S INN, LONDON, E.C.

TELEPHONE 14430 CENTRAL.

April 19 1912.

Dear Madam,

I am only one, only one, only one.
Only one being, one at the same time.
Not two, not three, only one. Only one
life to live, only sixty minutes in one
hour. Only one pair of eyes. Only one
brain. Only one being. Being only one,
having only one pair of eyes, having
only one time, having only one life, I
cannot read your M.S. three or four
times. Not even one time. Only one look,
only one look is enough. Hardly one
copy would sell here. Hardly one. Hardly
one.

Many thanks. I am returning the
M.S. by registered post. Only one M.S.
by one post.

Sincerely yours,

Miss Gertrude Stein,
  27 Rue de Fleurus,
      Paris,
        France.

I can't believe how hot you can be at night and
frigid in the morning.
I won't do this anymore;
I won't be one of your ridiculous lays.

From: Candace Walsh <

To: Melissa LaMunyon <melissa

Sent: Thursday, September 6, 200

Subject: Re: Query for a cleft lip

Dear Melissa,

We recently ran an article or

cleft palates, so we will pass

Best,
Candace

Candace Walsh
Articles Editor
Product Reviewer

@mothering.com

late personal essay

breastfeeding triplets with

on your query.

Jason,
    I guess I still sort of like Mike Stokes. It's not that I totally don't like you, it's just that there's other people that I've liked a longer time. I hope you're not real mad or anything. But I hope you still dance with me at the dance. Are you going? See ya there.
        Sorry . . .
            Luv Ya,
                Amy

it was kind of a joke. I like you ~~~~ But I really don't want to go with anyone right now, I'm not going to the dance

That's nice.

I guess your mad. I knew you still liked mike but it wasnt the slightest bit funny. So I just wanted to know what you would say! HAHA

Jason WB

and I know you werent totally joking because and besides I can tell. But whatever! —amy WB

December 20, 2007

Diana ▓▓▓▓▓
▓▓▓▓▓ Ave.
Davis, CA 9561▓

Re: Childcare Biting Incidents

Dear Diana,

Yesterday I wrote a letter that I was going to mail to you today concerning your child ▓▓▓▓ and three biting incidents. I am out in a seminar today and got a call from my childcare informing me that ▓▓▓▓ had bitten another child which makes it four times that she has done this.

Our policy states that the child is not to be allowed back in Childcare after the third incident. I was willing to be as reasonable as I could but after the fourth incident, ▓▓▓▓ will not be allowed in Childcare until July 1, 2008. At that time she will be allowed to stay as long as there is not another incident. If there is another incident we will evaluate the amount of time she won't be allowed in.

It is regrettable that I have to do this, but all of our members have to have the assurance that their children will be safe at all times when they are left in our care.

Sincerely,   -

Chris Raber
Owner

REACH YOUR PEAK

December 17, 1990

Arthur Gonzalez
3038 Texas Street
Oakland, CA 94602

Art Matters Inc.
131 West 24th Street
New York, N.Y. 10011
Tel. (212) 929-7190

Dear Arthur Gonzalez:

A large number of applications and restricted funding made decision-making at our recent meeting extremely difficult, and we were unable to make a grant to you for the work proposed.

Given that your work is known and admired by various people associated with AMI, we want to make sure you are aware of our respect for what you do, and to convey our sincere regret that we are unable to help you at this time.

All best wishes as you pursue your work. If it seems that there are other ways in which we can assist you, I hope you will contact our office. Your visual support materials will be returned to you by January 12, 1991.

Sincerely,

Laura Donnelley
President

ARTHUR ROGER

Dear Arthur,

Thank you for sending your portfolio. I enjoyed viewing it. Katherine Chapin was in the gallery the week earlier and showed us reproductions. She is very enthusiastic about your work and although I also find it — beautiful I am unable to fit it into our program at this time.

Best,
Arthur Roger

136 PRINCE STREET NEW YORK, NEW YORK 10012

THE NEW FIGURE/GROUND Relationship.

Bumpler 89

G.P.-S. 017-0127

BI-1694

DEPARTMENT: HOME AFFAIRS
REPUBLIC OF SOUTH AFRICA

NOTICE OF REFUSAL OF ENTRY INTO THE REPUBLIC OF SOUTH AFRICA

[Section 34 (8) of Act No. 13 of 2002: Regulation 39 (13)]

To: *Sanchez Garcia : Jorge Juan*

You are in terms of the provisions of sections *29 (1), 30 (1), 34 (8) of the Immigration Act, 2002 (Act No. 13 of 2002), refused admission to the Republic of South Africa as you—

- *(a) are a prohibited person; or
- *(b) are an undesirable person; or
- *(c) are an illegal foreigner as you are not in possession of a valid passport and/or a valid visa; or
- *(d) have failed to comply with the examination procedure.

In terms of section 34 (9) (c) of the said Act the conveyor responsible for your conveyance

to the Republic, namely...
will be responsible for your maintenance and removal from the RSA.

In terms of section 8 (5) of the Act, this decision is effective notwithstanding any further representations from you or on your behalf, and final for purposes of your removal/return to your country of origin.

After your removal/return to your country of origin you may, within 20 days from date of this notice, appeal to the Director-General of Home Affairs against this decision. Such an appeal must be lodged via the nearest or most convenient South African diplomatic or consular representative.

Date ...07/07/15...

....
Immigration Officer

Place ...Cpe Town...

I acknowledge receipt of the original of this notice

Jorge Sánchez

....
Signature of inadmissible person

Date: Mon, Jul 30, 2007 at 12:47 PM
Subject: Re: Nyc

I'm not really sure why you're contacting me, especially if you really feel that "something's missing." And I don't need my keys. Throw them out.

August 23, 1938

Mr. Joseph Bazzeghin
2131 Whitney Avenue
Hamden, Connecticut

Dear Sir:

This will acknowledge your several letters in
regard to the operation of a Cable Coaster on the
San Francisco-Oakland Bay Bridge during the 1939 Golden
Gate Exposition.

There are several objections to your proposal.
A sufficient one is the fact that the cars on the coaster
moving at the speeds you propose would so distract the
attention of the operators of motor vehicles on the bridge
as to increase the probability of accident. On this
ground alone, we would be forced to reject your proposal.

Very truly yours,

C. H. Purcell
Chief Engineer

By   ORIGINAL SIGNED BY
        CHAS. E. ANDREW

Chas. E. Andrew
Bridge Engineer

cc-Harry Hopkins

GBW

THE PUTNAM PUBLISHING GROUP, INC.

200 MADISON AVENUE · NEW YORK, NEW YORK 10016 · (212) 576-8900 · TELEX 42-2386 COMAGAN

KAREN R. MAYER
VICE PRESIDENT
GENERAL COUNSEL

(212) 576-8825

October 29, 1986

Mr. Matthew Eric Martin
18 Martinwood Drive
Erie, Pennsylvania 16509

Dear Mr. Martin:

Thank you for your interest in The Putnam Publishing Group.

Unfortunately, at this time there are no openings in our Legal Department. I will, however, keep your resume on file for future reference.

Best wishes in your search for the right position.

Sincerely,

Karen Mayer

Karen R. Mayer

KRM/as

P.S. Perhaps I may be able to call you in a few months.

*Matt
Sounds encouraging.
Call her in Jan.
Love Dad*

G. P. PUTNAM'S SONS · THE PUTNAM YOUNG READERS GROUP · THE BERKLEY PUBLISHING GROUP

NAME _Julie_

I can

	Yes	No
put my chin in the water..................	✓	
put my nose in the water..................	✓	
put my eyes in the water..................	✓	
put my WHOLE HEAD in the water...........	✓	
blow bubbles.............................	✓	
pick an object off of the bottom.........	✓	
hold my breath for _5_ seconds...........	✓	
do a face float while holding on to wall..		✓
face float while holding onto my teacher and/or the kick board..................	some	

Other. _Back float w/ help_

TIFICATE....

PASS TO II Seal Pup _____
Remain at I Water Frog ☒

Comments _Julie does very well_
in the water. She only
has to improve her face
float to go to Seal Pup II.

Instructor: _Ken Scherfee_

I. WATER FROG

NAME Julia

I can

	Yes	No
put my chin in the water....................	✓	
put my nose in the water....................	✓	
put my eyes in the water....................	✓	
put my WHOLE HEAD in the water............	✓	
blow bubbles..............................	✓	
pick an object off of the bottom..........	✓	
hold my breath for _11_ seconds............		✓
do a face float while holding on to wall..	✓	
face float while holding onto my teacher and/or the kick board..................	✓	

Other...........

CERTIFICATE....

PASS TO II Seal Pup _____
Remain at I Water Frog ✓

Comments <u>Julie need a little</u>
<u>help on a face to float</u>
<u>her feet wants to go to</u>
<u>the bottom of the Pool</u>

Instructor: <u>Laurie Henderson</u>

NAME Jolie

I can

	Yes	No
put my chin in the water.....................	✓	
put my nose in the water.....................	✓	
put my eyes in the water.....................	✓	
put my WHOLE HEAD in the water..............	✓	
blow bubbles.................................	✓	
pick an object off of the bottom...........	✓	
hold my breath for ____ seconds............	✓	
do a face float while holding on to wall..	✓	
face float while holding onto my teacher and/or the kick board..................	✓	

Other............

RTIFICATE....

PASS TO II Seal Pup ~~no~~ no
Remain at I Water Frog ✓

Comments *Still needs help on*

face float

_____

_____

Instructor: *Laurie Henderson*

May 21, 1942

Mr. J. L. Warner,
Warner Brothers,
Burbank, California

Dear Mr. Warner:

We have received Part II, also pages of
changes dated May 19th, for your proposed picture
CASABLANCA. As we indicated before, we cannot, of
course, give you a final opinion until we receive
the complete script.

However, the present material contains certain elements which seem to be unacceptable from the
standpoint of the Production Code. Specifically, we
cannot approve the present suggestion that Capt.
Renault makes a practice of seducing the women to
whom he grants visas. Any such inference of illicit
sex could not be approved in the finished picture.

Going through this new material, we call
your attention to the following:

Pages 70 and 71: The dialogue in scenes
125 and 126 is unacceptable by reason of its sex sug-
gestiveness.

Page 76: The following dialogue is unacceptable for the above reasons "By the way - another
visa problem has come up"; "Show her in".

Page 85: The line "You'll find it worth
your while" is unacceptably sex suggestive.

Page 86: The suggestion that Ilsa was married all the time she was having her love affair with
Rick in Paris seems unacceptable, and could not be
approved in the finished picture. Hence, we request
the deletion of Ilsa's line "Even when I knew you in
Paris".

We will be happy to read the balance of the
script, and to report further, whenever you have it
ready.

Cordially yours,

Joseph I. Breen

2:S

Dear Mommy,

can you please play with me? or go on a bike ride

love olivia

rit yes or no here

not right now.

rite a note

please ask daddy. :)

Sent: Sunday, August 10, 2008 6:53 AM
To:
Subject: Sharing some news

Dear Mom

I have not been in touch because I needed to wait in order to tell you
something major that's happening in my life...and to do this, it is
impossible for me to have much contact with you--my experience of being
your child is why it's taken me until almost 40 to become I a parent. I am
22-plus weeks pregnant with a little boy we're naming Lars Benjamin.

We'll let you know when he arrives.

Rachel

Michael Hearst

On 1/11/03 4:38 PM, "Michael Hearst" <▓▓▓▓▓@infi.net> wrote:

Hi Michael,

I hope you survived the holidays. Just checkin in on you to see if you were still interested in coming up with some lyrics. To give you an update, we have finsihed songs for Dave Eggers, Rick Moody, Daniel Handler, Mary Gaitskillis, Clay McLeod Chapman, Lawrence Krauser, Amy Fusselman, A.M. Homes, Neil Gaiman, Darin Strauss, Jonathan Lethem and Paul Auster.
  Today we are working on Myla Goldberg's piece. Auster is actually bringing his 16 yr old daughter, Sophie over tomorrow to sing on Myla's song. Apparently she has an amazing voice. I love it!
Anyway, we would still be completely honored if you could throw some lyrics our way.

all the best,
Michael Hearst

Michael Hearst / One Ring Zero
http://www.oneringzero.com

Dear Michael,

I'm sorry, I just can't seem to get it together to focus on this right now. I'm really sorry to be left out of such a distinguished group. I suck!

MC

F C
F F△5 B♭ C♯ F A B♭ C♯
C B♭ F F/E Dm B♭ C♯ F C

July 8 , 2004

Dear Craig,

Thank you very much for your interest in *According to Jim*.

You were strongly considered in our final group of candidates. I was very impressed with your interviewing skills and your positive attitude. It is unfortunate that we only had one position available.

Regrettably, we have offered the position to someone else. We will keep your resume on file with hopes that we may work together in the future.

Best Regards,

Bob Heath
Bob Heath
Producer

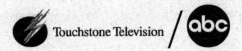

CBS STUDIO CENTER 4024 RADFORD AVENUE STUDIO CITY, CA 91604

ROBERT A. LURIE
PRESIDENT

August 10, 1984

Mr. Danny Brown
8811 Poplar Avenue
Cotati, CA 94928

Dear Mr. Brown:

Thank you for your recent letter and interest in the Giants and in the job of field manager.

At this time, while it was an extremely difficult decision to let Frank Robinson go, I am glad we are able to draw upon proven resources within our own organization, like Danny Ozark, to put together a respectable finish for the end of the season and to set a new winning attitude for the future.

Your own determination and genuine love for the Game may, with added experience, lead you to the kind of job you want someday. At this point, however, I do not believe you possess the qualifications for the job of field manager.

I do appreciate your interest and especially your loyal support of the Giants.

Sincerely,

Robert A. Lurie
President

RAL/fm

August 27, 1997

Dear Jed,

I assume that since I haven't heard from you I'm not a priority in your life. This makes me angry and sad but I think it's the right thing for both of us. I can't do this any longer. The experience of being with you occasionally isn't worth the frustration and upset I feel from it. You've been telling me all along that you don't have the ability to be involved in a relationship but enjoy my company from time to time. You also said that I needed to decide when I'd had enough of our "casual arrangement". I've been listening but not really getting the message until now. Somehow, your life swallows you up so that you can't let anybody in close. Personally, I think you are missing out on a great opportunity with me, but of course I have a bias.

It's best for me not to be involved with you anymore. I have to say that it's probably best for you not to date me let alone any other woman until you are ready to go to some kind of deeper level with another human being.

I hope you know how much I care about you. Not only are you an amazing man, but you have profoundly touched my life. You've taught me more than you even know about myself, life, and the ways of the world. Thank you for being a part of my journey. I have no doubt that we'll bump into each other again in the future and look forward to that meeting. Please take good care of yourself.   Know that in my own way I love you dearly.

You don't have to respond if you don't want, except to let me know that you got this message.

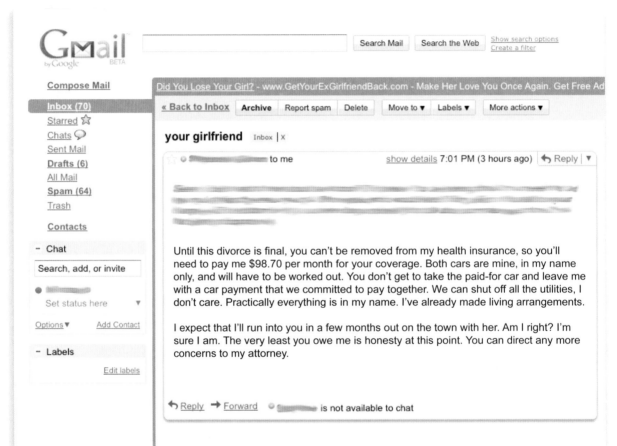

Until this divorce is final, you can't be removed from my health insurance, so you'll need to pay me $98.70 per month for your coverage. Both cars are mine, in my name only, and will have to be worked out. You don't get to take the paid-for car and leave me with a car payment that we committed to pay together. We can shut off all the utilities, I don't care. Practically everything is in my name. I've already made living arrangements.

I expect that I'll run into you in a few months out on the town with her. Am I right? I'm sure I am. The very least you owe me is honesty at this point. You can direct any more concerns to my attorney.

↩ Reply   → Forward   ● ▓▓▓▓▓▓ is not available to chat

ANtho...ng

thanks For the BOOK.
REALLY NICE WORK.

SORRY, BUT NOT This
Time

———————→ Steve Byram

IN CASE
YOU DID
NOT NOTICE
THIS IS
EMPLOYEE
PARKING.
THAT MEANS
<u>YOU</u> DONT
PARK HERE.
NEXT TIME
YOU WILL
BE TOWED.
WE KNOW
YOUR CAR
THANKS
-OTP

NICE PARKING

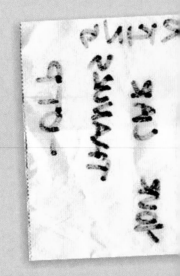

IN CASE YOU DID NOT
NOTICE I WAS IN YOUR
RESTURANT WITH 4 CLAMS
WHICH WILL NEVER
HAPPAN AGAIN. I
KNOW WHO YOU ARE TOO!

__31 May 62__
(Date)

SUBJECT: Request for Discharge

TO: Commanding Officer
       101st Airborne Support Group
       101st Airborne Division

1. Recommend the following named enlisted man be:

  X_ Discharged under authority contained in AR 635-208.

  ___ Discharged under authority contained in AR 635-209.

Hendrix, James M	RA 19 693 532	Pvt E-2	HQ & Co "A", 801st Maint Bn Spt GP, 101st Abn Div
(Name)	(SN)	(Grade)	(Organization)

2. Age _19_

3. Date of (*enlistment) (~~*induction~~) _May 61_

4. Term for which (*enlisted) (~~*inducted~~) _3 years_

5. Prior service _None_

6. This enlisted man (~~*does~~) (*does not) have a reserve commission or warrant. (If so, show service number, grade, and date of appointment).

7. Reasons for the action recommended: (General nondescriptive terms will be avoided) Behavior problems, requires excessive supervision while on duty, little regard for regulations, apprehended masturbating in platoon area while supposed to be on detail.

8. AFQT score: _54_

9. Aptitude area scores: CO-A_120_; CO-B_109_; EL_106_; _M_117_; MM _93_; CL_114_; GT_109_; RC_121_; IN___; AE _._

10. Conduct rating _Uns_ Efficiency rating _Unc_
Duty MOS _760.07_ PMOS _760.07_ .

*Line out words not applicable.

FC FL 603(Rev)
27 Mar 62

STATEMENT
(AR 190-45)

PLACE	DATE	FILE NO.
Fort Campbell, Kentucky	28 May 1962	
DEPONENT (Last Name -- First Name - Middle Initial)	SERVICE NO.	GRADE
Hoekstra, Louis J	RA 16 227 362	1st Sgt E-8

ORGANIZATION (If deponent is a civilian, give address)

HQ & Co "A", 801st Maint Bn, Spt GP, 101st Abn Div

I HAVE BEEN INFORMED BY __Capt Gilbert R Batchman__, WHO STATED HE IS *(a)* XXX
Commissioned Officer _____, OF THE UNITED STATES *(Army)* XXXXXXXXXXXXXXXXX,
THAT HE IS CONDUCTING AN INVESTIGATION OF __208 Board Proceedings__,
XXXXXXXXXXXXXXXXXXXXXXXXXXXXXXXXXXX*Strike out words between brackets, if inapplicable).*

"THE UNIFORM CODE OF MILITARY JUSTICE, ARTICLE 31, XXXXXXXXXXXXXXXXXXXXXXXXXXXXX
XXXXXXXXXXXXXXXXXXXXXXXXXXXXXX*(Strike out only if person making statement IS a member of the Armed Forces) (has)* XXXXXXX BEEN READ TO ME BY____Capt Batchman____.
I UNDERSTAND THAT I DO NOT HAVE TO MAKE ANY STATEMENT WHATSOEVER AND ANY STATEMENT I MAKE
MAY BE USED AS EVIDENCE AGAINST ME."

I have known Pvt James M Hendrix, RA 19 693 532, since he was assigned to the
Unit in Nov 61. He was assigned to the Repair Parts Section for duty as a supply
clerk. Shortly after his assignment his section Sgt, Sgt Bowman, came to me and
indicated that Hendrix was going to be a problem. I have since then found that
Hendrix is poorly motivated for the military, has no regard for regulations, requires excessive supervision while performing his duties, pays no heed to counsel-
ing from his supervisors as to his shortcomings. He is a habitual offender when it
comes to making bed check, having missed bed check in March, April and May.
    Hendrix has been counseled regarding his shortcomings at extreme lengths by
Capt Gilbert R Batchman, to no avail. At times Hendrix isn't able to carry on an
intelligent conversation, paying little attention to having been spoken to. At
one point it was thought perhaps Hendrix was taking dope and was sent to be ex-
amined by a medical officer with negative results. He has been undergoing group
therapy at Mental Hygeine with negative results.
    Pvt Hendrix plays a musical instrument during his off duty hours, or so he
says. This is one of his faults, because his mind apparently cannot function
while performing duties and thinking about his guitar.
    On 23 May 62, Hendrix missed bed check, also at that time his pass privileges
were withdrawn by the company commander. However Hendrix will readily admit to being off post without a pass, showing no regard for regulations.
    I recommend with out hesitancy that Hendrix be eliminated from the service
under the provisions of AR 635-208 as expeditious as possible.

EXHIBIT	DEPONENT'S INITIALS	PAGE 1 OF 2 PAGES

"MY PARENTS HATE ME TOO!
what I want to d.
I'M NO
HAPPY
messy room
Smiles
peace
cool clothes
good food
swim

what they want me to do

clean room

spanking

frowns

dorky clothes

gross food

BAbysit

Joyce,

Paul told me about your talk last night. I am so sad we have reached this pass. You might think this could all have been avoided had I never, ever talked to him. Perhaps. Before you + I say goodbye, I need to tell you some things:

① I would not have chased your ex-husband. He is pursuing me.

② Now that you are happily living with someone new, I feel that Paul + I have the right to get to know each other.

③ It grieves me that this hurts you.

I need to take this path for my own life. I wish you well with yours — Meg

THE OPRAH
MAGAZINE

Dear Reader:

Thank you so much for sharing your ideas with us. Unfortunately, due to the sheer volume of material we have at hand, we are unable to incorporate your concept. We wish you much success in placing your work elsewhere, and we thank you for your interest in *O, The Oprah Magazine.*

Sincerely,

The Editors

February 26, 1939.

My dear Mrs. Henry M. Robert: Jr

I am afraid that I have never been a very
useful member of the Daughters of the
American Revolution, so I know it will
make very little difference to you whether
I resign, or whether I continue to be a
member of your organization.

However, I am in complete disagreement
with the attitude taken in refusing
Constitution Hall to a great artist.
You have set an example which seems to
me unfortunate, and I feel obliged to
send in to you my resignation.   You
had an opportunity to lead in an enligh-
tened way and it seems to me that your
organization has failed.

I realize that many people will not agree
with me, but feeling as I do this seems
to me the only proper procedure to
follow.

                Very sincerely yours,

March 27, 1990

To my friends at Carsey-Werner Company, ABC, to the cast, crew and staff of "Roseanne":

My sincere and heartfelt thanks to all of you.

I have chosen not to return to the show next season. Instead, my wife and I have decided to share a vacation in the relative peace and quiet of Beirut.

JEFF HARRIS
Executive Producer

National Aeronautics and
Space Administration

Lyndon B. Johnson Space Center
2101 NASA Road 1
Houston, Texas 77058-3696

Reply to Attn of AHX   May 7, 1996

Mr. Clayton C. Anderson
1909 Summer Reef Drive
League City, TX 77573

Dear Clay:

Thank you for applying for the Astronaut Candidate Program.

We certainly regretted having to inform you that you were not selected for the
Program.

Twenty-five mission specialist and ten pilot astronaut candidates were selected from
over 2,400 applicants. Competition for the program was again extremely keen, and
the limited number of openings precluded many highly-qualified individuals, such as
yourself, from being selected.

We appreciate the opportunity to interview you for the Astronaut Candidate Program
and wish you success in your future endeavors.

Sincerely,

Duane L. Ross
Manager, Astronaut Selection Office

Amy,
OK I'll stop saying things about your butt. What did you think i like you as a girlfriend well I dont ok

By
Mike

I just cant do it. I believe that you want to be with me now, but I don't believe that you will in three months, or even one. You know it breaks my heart, because there is nothing more that Ive wanted than to be with you since may ... but ████ i am wrung dry. i am worn out ... im tired, and i still feel broken. and i want to hit you and throw things at you and scream that you're an idiot for not seeing me for who i am sooner ...

Recruitment Center

April 18, 2007

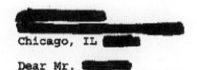

Chicago, IL ████

Dear Mr. ████

Thank you for your interest in the CST Division. As our representative explained to you, competition for employment is very keen at this time because we have an abundance of qualified people applying for the limited number of positions available. We have reviewed your qualifications, and unfortunately we do not have a position to offer you at this time.

Our recruiter enjoyed talking with you and regrets that our response could not be more favorable. We thank you for your interest in Agency employment and wish you the best of luck in your future endeavors.

Sincerely,

Chief, CST Division

I HAT YOU FROM

PHOEBE

years bring new retrospectives about the lives of Jack and Bobby Kennedy, but self-congratulation for surviving five years in the publishing business? On this special issue, we'd give *EW* an F.

—FEBRUARY 21

THE MAIL
★

NYPress *encourages submissions to The Mail. Letters must address past articles in NYPress or topics of interest to readers living or working in Manhattan. Please include name, address and daytime phone number. Send all correspondence to: The Mail, NYPress, The Puck Bldg., 295 Lafayette St., NYC 10012. Fax: 212-941-7824. E-mail via Internet: 71632.16@compuserve.com.*

Crass Transit

I WAS GLAD TO SEE THE LITTLE SQUIB ON the front page of last week's issue about the problems on the 4, 5 and 6 subway lines.

This is exactly the kind of thing that never shows up in any other paper. What compels me to write, however, is the New York phenomenon of bitterness...that makes me have to point out to the squib writer that *I hate you*.

Why? Because, I was further down the line at Astor Pl. at the *same exact time as you*. I never received any announcement about the delays (garbled or otherwise)...and when at last the "rush-hour crowded" train appeared in the tube, it sped right past Astor Pl. probably containing *you*. Since the Transit Authority is immune I have no choice but to blame you.

—J.T. COLFAX, BROOKLYN

Resume on File Dept.

WAS SAM SIFTON STARING AT A MIRROR in Milano's, as his review of the bar would seem to suggest? For a paper as commercially ironic as *NYPress*, the criticism of Mont Blanc-wielding boys in paint-spattered chinos hanging out downmarket sounds suspiciously close to your collective editorial, all white, Ivy League bone. One surmises that Harvard boys in their late 20s who get work at a freebie advertising circular are not made any more interesting by a display of self-hatred written (and I use the word lightly) in the third person.

—WILLIAM J. GEORGIADES, MANHATTAN

Sam Sifton replies: For the record, I am the only Ivy League graduate on the NYPress *staff. Speaking collectively, though, one wonders if any of Georgiades' bitterness stems from the fact that he has attempted to secure work as a writer here three times in the past year, each time unsuccessfully.*

Hill Billy

STRANGE THAT MUGGER SHOULD COMMEND Hendrik Hertzberg of *The New Yorker* (*NYPress*, 2/8) for writing a single positive sentence about Newt Gingrich. Unlike MUGGER, Hertzberg is a thinker and not a propagandist.

In roughly three years of columns has MUGGER ever heaped anything but abuse upon Bill and Hillary Clinton? He even blames our president for not settling the baseball strike. Isn't pro sports the sort of non-essential entertainment a lean government like Gingrich favors should keep its nose out of?

—KENNETH HERMANN, MANHATTAN

Frosted Flake

I AM NOT ONE WHO NORMALLY TAKES TIME out to write to periodicals. Jeez, I'd be lucky if I could find the time to write to my own relatives. Nonetheless, I would like to take this opportunity to compliment and thank all of you for the wonderful weekly service that you provide to faithful readers such as myself.

For the past three years of my 20-year existence, I have religiously read *NYPress*. As an adolescent I cannot remember anything else that I ever did religiously! *NYPress* repre-

»

PLAYBOY

Dear Candidate:

Thank you for submitting your pictures to PLAYBOY. The editors have viewed them and carefully considered your potential for Playmate of the Month

While you are certainly an attractive young lady, we are unable to accept you as a candidate for this feature. The competition for Playmate is very keen and we must, unfortunately, turn down many lovely candidates.

We do appreciate your sending us the pictures and thinking of PLAYBOY.

Sincerely,

The Editors

Chicago, Ill., September 28, 1920.

To:

Charles Risberg,
Fred McMullin,
Joe Jackson,
Oscar Felsch,
George Weaver,
C.P.Williams and
E.V.Cicotte:

You and each of you are hereby notified of your indefinite suspension as a member of the Chicago American League Base-Ball Club (the White Sox).

Your suspension is brought about by information which has just come to me directly involving you and each of you in the base-ball scandal (now being investigated by the present Grand Jury of Cook County) resulting from the World's Series of 1919.

If you are innocent of any wrong doing you and each of you will be reinstated; if you are guilty you will be retired from organized base-ball for the rest of your lives, if I can accomplish it.

Until there is a finality to this investigation it is due to the public that I take this action even though it costs Chicago the pennant.

CHICAGO AMERICAN LEAGUE BASEBALL CLUB,

By _____

Literary Agency

Zoe

Dear Author:

Thank you for your submission. *query*

We appreciate the opportunity to review your work. Please be assured that your manuscript has been read and thoroughly evaluated. Regrettably it did not seem right for this agency, but this rejection does not reflect on its merit.

This is a subjective business and anothe[r]
differently. We wish you much luc[k]

Sincerely,

• Suite 5
TEL: 858.755.8761 • FA[X]

THE AXELROD AGEN[CY]

55 M[ain]
P.O.
Chatham, New [York]

Thank you for contacting us.

We are sorry to say that due to commit[ment]
prese[nt]s we cannot offer to read [your]
[lu]ck in your s[earch]

We
re

STERLING L[ORD]

65 Bleecker Street • New Y[ork]

March 9, 2008

Dear Zoe Gayl,

Thank you for your recent query let[ter]
seems a rich and rollicking one. Unf[ortunately]
confident of this novel's commercia[l]
agent for your work.

Best wishes,

Jean V. Naggar Literary Agency, Inc.

Dear Author,

Thank you for giving me the opportunity to consider y[our]
I have read your query, but do not think I would be th[e]
I wish I could have responded personally to every inqu[iry]
but the volume of mail I receive makes it impossible.

Good luck in your search for the appropriate agent and
your work.

Sincerely,

Mollie Glick

RATED

ENUE, NEW YORK, N.Y. 10017

CIATES

We are sorry but our client list is already so long and the work on hand so heavy that we don't feel justified in adding to it.

Thank you for writing to us.

February 27, 2008

Zoe Gayl

Santa Fe, NM 87

Dear Ms. Gayl:

ank you for your recent submission.

le we do think there is a market for your work, unfortunately, we're just
he right agency to take it on. We feel we must be 100% behind a
ct in order to sell in this extremely difficult market. We just can't see
y to representing this without being confident that we could make a
le for you.

I wish you much success in your search for the right agent and thanks again

o our
aterial.

or

D LITERISTIC, INC.

12 • (212) 780-6050 • FAX (212) 780-6095

ng your novel, *Right Church*.... Your s
though, in the end we are not sufficient
in a difficult marketplace to be the right

Meredith Bernstein Literary Agency
2095 Broadway suite 505
New York, N.Y. 10023

Thank you for your query to our agency.

Due to the current status of the publishing
industry--and the selectivity that the market
now demands, we regret that we cannot
consider your material at this time.

best wishes for success in publishing.

ith Bernstein

TRUMP
THE TRUMP ORGANIZATION

March 21, 2005

Mr. Gregory Garry
Director of Photography
Budget Living Magazine
665 Broadway, 9th Floor
New York, NY 10012

Dear Mr. Garry:

The Trump Organization is in receipt of your letter dated March 4, 2005.

While the Best Buy section of Budget Living magazine looks great and is obviously a big success, regretfully, Mr. Trump will not be able to pose for a layout at this time. His schedule is just too overbooked right now. Thank you for considering Mr. Trump for this endeavor --- perhaps we can work together sometime in the future.

With best wishes,

Sincerely,

Norma Foerderer
Vice President

HOW COME I'M NOT RESPONDING
TO YOUR LETTER?

BECAUSE I DO NOT WANT TO BE
WITH YOU. NOT NOW. NOT EVER.
AND NOT JUST FRIENDS. NOT
ANYTHING.

SO CAN WE JUST STOP THIS?

November 6, 2008

Will,

The past few weeks have been hard for both of us, & I
wanted to make sure that you understood my desision.
Believe me, it was not easy. After months of flirting &
getting to know each other, & weeks of anticipating
a first kiss I too, am surprised that my mind jumped
on me so fast. I still am not sure if I even know,
really, why. I haven't been completely honest or fair
towards you, when you deserve all the respect in the
world. I realize that I led you on. It was incredibly
bitchy, & I did not realize, as hard as it is to believe,
that I was doing so. I kept telling myself how
much I liked you, & believe me I did (& still do,)
but I was right when I say that I simply was
not feeling it. In the back of my mind I knew
that it was wrong. My heart is still tender, & cries
at the thought of my past. As unfortunate as it is,
I simply am not ready to be involved in another
relationship as serious as my previous one was. I need
time to collect my thoughts a bit more, & experience the
feeling one gets when they are alone, with no one to turn
to, so my heart can figure out how to be productive &
deal with it. I want to make sure that you know
that I did have fun with you, & still want to be very
close friends. If you've learned anything about me
you will know that I keep my friends (especially the
guys) extremely close. You are one of these guys, will.
we don't need to have that ridiculous title to stay
close & have fun, though right now it may seem like

that would be a difficult thing. I guess that what I am really trying to say, Will, is that I'm sorry. You may not want to forgive me now, but I ask that someday you will. It feels horrible, I know, to have something so great end so suddenly, but what exactly is ending? The ability to have a formal title expressing to those who listen the feelings that two people have for eachother? To me, it is far more special when those listeners hear nothing, but have the intuitive gift to notice something as powerful as a friendship so discreetly. Will, I am so glad that I have gotten to know you as well as I have. I hope that now you are able to understand why I made the abrupt desicion that I did, + once again I am sorry. I really do hope to stay close in the near future.
Thank you, for a wonderful few months.

Yours,

Zoe

CALIFORNIA OFFICE OF REAL ESTATE APPRAISERS

CAT0540

ROSLYN

DAVIS

CA   95616

SSN:

DOB: / /1965

Candidate ID: CA2222086760

Examination: **Certified Residential Appraiser**

Exam Result: **FAIL**

Exam Date: **12/15/2007**

We regret to inform you that you have not passed the appraiser examination. The diagnostic report below shows your performance in each of the general knowledge content areas. Please consult the National Uniform Appraiser Examination Candidate Handbook and the California Test Center and Fee Card for additional information about the examination and procedures.

If you wish to retake the examination you must complete the Request for Re-examination form (REA 3007). This form must be obtained from the test center manager. Send the complete form to:

Office of Real Estate Appraisers
1102 Q Street, Suite 4100
Sacramento, CA 95814

Diagnostic Report

Passing Score: 75   Your Score: 71

Content Areas

High

Low

I, II, III

IV, V

VI, VII, VIII, IX

X, XI

XII

XIII

XIV, XV

TEXAS INSTRUMENTS

TER'S DIRECT PHONE NO.:
ECOPIER NO.: (214) 995-3511

December 5, 1988

Mr. Rich Barrett
P. O. Box 9241
Pittsburgh, PA 15224

Ref. Our File No. 88-0434

Dear Mr. Barrett:

We have now completed our review of the information you sent us suggesting three ideas: Chemical Cal, Magnetic Pollinater, and Smell Detector.

Although our reviewers found your ideas interesting, we have decided not to use your suggestions.

We would like you to know how much we appreciate your interest in Texas Instruments, and thank you for giving us the opportunity to consider your ideas.

Sincerely yours,

Gary C. Honeycutt
Division Patent Counsel
Texas Instruments Incorporated
P. O. Box 655474, MS 219
Dallas, Texas 75265

GCH:hw

PC-A-6

March 16, 1998

Dear Mr. Barrett:

I want to thank you for sharing your album and letters concerning your study of the INSANITY OF WAR. Given the amount of time you've spent on it, I'm returning it for safe keeping

Please accept, in return of your generous gesture, my best wishes to you and good luck in all that you do.

Cordially,

51 WEST 52 STREET
NEW YORK, NEW YORK 10019-6188

Dear Mr. Barrett,   November 13, 1998

Enclosed, please find your notebook entitled 'The Insanity of War.' We apologize for the long delay in responding, but Mr. Cronkite has been out of the office a great deal this year. In fact, Mr. Cronkite could not respond personally as he is out of the office for the next several weeks.

Mr. Cronkite asked me to extend his deepest regrets that there is not more that he can do for you in your quest to receive full disability from the Veterans Administration. Mr. Cronkite has publicly condemned the governments handling of the Vietnam War for over twenty years, and sympathizes with your plight. However, due to the inordinate amount of material of this nature he receives, it is impossible for him to respond to every request, no matter how worthy.

Thus, he has asked me to return your notebook so that it may be submitted to other parties in the future.

Mr. Cronkite thanks you for thinking of him, and hopes for a positive conclusion to your dilemma.

Sincerely,

Sterling Rome
Assistant to Walter Cronkite

TEXAS AND SOUTHWESTERN CATTLE RAISERS ASSOCIATION

1301 W. SEVENTH ST. FORT WORTH, TEXAS 76102-2665 817-332-7064 FAX 817-332-6441

JOHN E. DUDLEY, PRESIDENT   BOB MCCAN, 1ST VICE PRESIDENT   C.R. "DICK" SHERRON, 2ND VICE PRESIDENT

MATT BROCKMAN, EXECUTIVE VICE PRESIDENT   FAX 817-338-4813

Mr. Richard Barrett
506 Walnut Street
Pittsburgh, PA 15238

Dear Mr. Barrett:

This is to acknowledge receipt of the photos and letters you sent us. We have reviewed the material and are unsure of your purpose in sending it to us, so we are returning it to you for safekeeping.

Sincerely,

CAROLYN A. JOHNSON
Administrative Assistant / Event Coordinator

CJ:klh
Enclosure

PUBLISHERS OF *The Cattleman*

June 27, 1988

Mr. Richard Barrett
P.O. Box 9241
Pittsburgh, PA   15224

Ref: N. D. File #244793

Dear Mr. Barrett:

Our New Devices Section received your disclosure of June 4, 1988 concerning a sliding wedge disc brake and a light analyzer, your correspondence postmarked June 14, 1988 containing various non-automotive proposals and your correspondence of June 20, 1988 consisting of a number of literary compositions.

We have reviewed the information provided on your proposed sliding wedge disc brake and the light analyzer. It was determined that General Motors would not be interested in acquiring the rights to any patented or patentable features which may exist in your proposed arrangements.

We regret our reply could not be favorable. However, we appreciate your interest in General Motors. Thank you.

Very truly yours,

N. B. Budzol
Senior Design Engineer
GM New Devices Section

pt

The Royal Hashemite Court

Amman
October 26th, 1997

Dear Mr Barrett,

His Majesty King Hussein I has commanded me to thank you for kindly sharing your interesting album illustrating *"The Insanity of War"*. (We are returning your valuable album in case of need in the future).

On behalf of His Majesty, we send best wishes to you and your family.

Yours sincerely

Brigadier Ali Shukri
Director

Yale University

Office of Public Affairs
P.O. Box 208279
New Haven, Connecticut 06520-8279

Telephone: 203 432-1333
Fax: 203 432-1323

August 22, 2007

Dear Mr Barrett,

Thank you for sharing your proposal for a debate between Harvard and Yale. It is, indeed, a splendid idea, but it is, alas, outside our purview.

Thank you also for sending us your very impressive background information, which I am returning for your safe-keeping or possible re-use.

Good luck on this and future endeavors.

Best,

Dorie Baker
Associate Director
Public Affairs

SECRETARIAT OF STATE

FIRST SECTION · GENERAL AFFAIRS

From the Vatican, November 3, 1997

Dear Mr. Barrett,

The Holy Father has asked me to thank you for your kind gift. He very much appreciates your thoughtful gesture.

His Holiness will remember you in his prayers and he invokes upon you God's blessings of joy and peace.

Sincerely yours,

Monsignor J.M. Harvey
Assessor

McBastard

I lost count of how many times you have broken my heart. I've had enough, i'm tired of letting you hurt me. I know so much more than you can imagine and the fact that u can't man up to it upsets me. Unlike you, I can't

Options   Send   Back

pretend like everything is great between us cuz they're not and they won't ever be.

Options   **Send**   Back

Sent: Monday, July 09, 2007 10:44 AM
Subject: Re: The most beautiful rainbow

Dad,

If you can't say anything nice don't bother sending me an

email. Same words, different year. I didn't like the nasty messages then, I don't like them now. You dug your own grave, and seem to be still digging. I hope it is working out for you...

--Your former son

March 25, 2008

Ms. Haley Smernoff

Santa Monica, CA 90401

Dear Ms. Smernoff,

Thank you for sending us your manuscript entitled *Duck's Amazing Hero.* Unfortunately, we are going to have to pass on the opportunity to publish it. We receive many manuscripts from people whose lives have been touched by cancer each year and are inspired and encouraged by them. However, because of the small size of our book publishing group we are limited in the number of titles we can print and publish in any given year. Often, this means choosing from among many publishable manuscripts. And in fact, it is not uncommon for books turned down by us to find homes with other publishers.

I think this will be the case with your book, and I wish you all success.

Sincerely,

Len Boswell
Book Publishing Director

Enclosures: Resources for Authors
                101 Cancer Publishers

National Home Office
250 Williams Street NW Atlanta, GA 30303-1002
404.320.3333
Cancer Information   1.800.ACS.2345   www.cancer.org

Hope.Progress.Answers.

Dear Doofus kemle,
I HATE YoU
STUpid crap- ASS
Your an I diot!

P.S.

when youre a teen-
ager move to
India.

your **O L D**
friend,

ALEX

3

Telephone
MUrray Hill 2-0500

Chock full o' Nuts

425 LEXINGTON AVENUE

New York 17, N. Y.

May 13, 1958

The President
The White House
Washington, D. C.

My dear Mr. President:

I was sitting in the audience at the Summit Meeting of Negro
Leaders yesterday when you said we must have patience. On
hearing you say this, I felt like standing up and saying, "Oh
no! Not again."

I respectfully remind you sir, that we have been the most
patient of all people. When you said we must have self-
respect, I wondered how we could have self-respect and remain patient considering the treatment accorded us through
the years.

17 million Negroes cannot do as you suggest and wait for the
hearts of men to change. We want to enjoy now the rights
that we feel we are entitled to as Americans. This we cannot do unless we pursue aggressively goals which all other
Americans achieved over 150 years ago.

As the chief executive of our nation, I respectfully suggest
that you unwittingly crush the spirit of freedom in Negroes
by constantly urging forbearance and give hope to those pro-
segregation leaders like Governor Faubus who would take
from us even those freedoms we now enjoy. Your own experience with Governor Faubus is proof enough that forbearance and not eventual integration is the goal the pro-
segregation leaders seek.

In my view, an unequivocal statement backed up by action
such as you demonstrated you could take last fall in deal-

ing with Governor Faubus if it became necessary, would let
it be known that America is determined to provide -- in the
near future -- for Negroes -- the freedoms we are entitled to under the constitution.

Respectfully yours,

Jackie Robinson

Jackie Robinson

JR:cc

THE CHURCH OF
JESUS CHRIST
OF LATTER-DAY SAINTS

July 16, 2008

Chad Michael Hardy
_____ Street
Las Vegas, Nevada 89123

Dear Brother Hardy,

I express my sincere appreciation to you for attending the Stake Disciplinary Council held in your behalf on Sunday, July 13, 2008 at 3:00p. After careful and prayerful consideration of all matters, the decision of the council is that you be excommunicated from the Church for conduct unbecoming a member of the Church.

A person who is excommunicated does not enjoy any privileges of Church membership. Your name has been removed from the records of the Church. You may not wear temple garments or pay tithes and offerings. You may not perform or participate in any priesthood ordinations or associated responsibilities. You may attend public Church meetings, however you are not permitted to participate in any class discussion, hold any callings or participate in the sustaining of officers and teachers.

Brother Hardy, as you felt during the council, we have a sincere love for you and a concern for your spiritual well being and progression. It is my desire that you would give heart-felt consideration regarding your present status and do all that you can to return to the Church. The repentance process takes time and having been excommunicated, requires a minimum of one year.

NORM B. FINLINSON, PH.D.
Executive Director
Student Academic and Advisement Services

September 30, 2008

Mr. Chad Michael Hardy
PO Box 977
Las Vegas, NV 84193

Dear Mr. Hardy:

This correspondence is to inform you that your name has been deleted from the August 2008 Graduation list and you will not be awarded a degree from Brigham Young University. A non-academic hold was placed on your record prior to the posting of degrees. The University became aware that you were not in good honor code standing to graduate because you had been excommunicated from the Church of Jesus Christ of Latter-Day Saints, the affiliated sponsor of BYU.

Your graduation application will be placed in a "hold" file and your name will not be resubmitted for graduation. If in the future you are reinstated as a member of the Church in good standing, you are invited to contact my office regarding your possible eligibility for the awarding of a degree.

Sincerely,

Norman B. Finlinson
Executive Director,
Student Academic & Advisement Services

SPO

C: Michael R. Orme
   Janet S. Scharman
   Vernon L. Heperi
   Jeffery Bunker

DIN: 81A3860

INTERVIEW DATE: 10-05-2004

BOARD DATE: 10-04

INTERVIEW TYPE: REAPPEAR

NAME: CHAPMAN,MARK D

OWNING FACILITY: ATTICA

SCHEDULED FACILITY: ATTICA
 PRISON TIME: 278 MONTHS
 PREVIOUS HOLD: 24 MONTHS   EARNED ELIGIBILITY: INELIGIBLE

DECISION: DENIED - HOLD FOR 24 MONTHS, NEXT APPEARANCE DATE: 10/2006

 DECIDING COMMISSIONER: SMITH,W. WILLIAM JR.
 OTHER MEMBER(S): MANLEY,VERNON C.   LAZZARI,LIVIO

FOLLOWING A PERSONAL INTERVIEW, A REVIEW OF YOUR RECORDS, AND
DELIBERATION, YOUR RELEASE TO PAROLE SUPERVISION AT THIS TIME IS
DENIED. THIS IS BASED ON THE EXTREME MALICIOUS INTENT YOU EXHIBITED
DURING THE INSTANT OFFENSE WHERE YOU FIRED A HANDGUN MULTIPLE TIMES
STRIKING YOUR TARGET - JOHN LENNON.

YOUR COURSE OF CONDUCT OVER A LENGTHY PERIOD OF TIME SHOWS A CLEAR
LACK OF RESPECT FOR LIFE AND SUBJECTED THE WIFE OF THE VICTIM TO
MONUMENTAL SUFFERING BY HER WITNESSING THE CRIME.

YOUR LIMITED VIOLENCE AND ANGER PROGRAMMING DUE TO YOUR HOUSING
STATUS, AS WELL AS YOUR POSITIVE DISCIPLINARY RECORD HAVE BEEN
CONSIDERED.

DURING THE INTERVIEW YOUR STATEMENTS FOR MOTIVATION ACKNOWLEDGES THE
ATTENTION YOU FELT THIS MURDER WOULD GENERATE. ALTHOUGH PROVEN TRUE,
SUCH RATIONALE IS BIZARRE AND MORALLY CORRUPT.

TO RELEASE YOU ON PAROLE AT THIS TIME WOULD SIGNIFICANTLY UNDERMINE
RESPECT FOR THE LAW.

January 19, 2009

Dear ▓▓▓▓

As we have discussed in today's meeting, your position is being eliminated effective February 2, 2009.

In connection with the termination of your employment, we are offering you the following: You will receive a lump sum payment in an amount equal to two (2) months' base salary, less all applicable state and federal taxes and payroll withholdings, in exchange for a general release pursuant to the company's standard form of separation and release agreement. The agreement will also include a payment of $500.00 for you to use at your discretion for outplacement services. Your medical and dental benefits will end on February 28th, 2009 per the terms of our program. After that time, you will have the right to convert your health insurance benefits to individual coverage pursuant to COBRA at your own expense. Details regarding this benefit will be sent to you separately. All other benefits will end on February 2nd, including, but not limited to, life insurance, 401(k), and flex spending.

Flat Rock, North Carolina

January 7, 1946.

Dear Mrs. Herrick:

As an old Elmhurst resident who walked and bicycled through Wheaton a hundred times, it is with regret that I cannot find time in my schedule for a visit.

Believe me,

Sincerely yours,

Carl Sandburg

3 Burroughs Irvine, CA 92618

August 22, 2005

Dear Ms. Lieberman,

I have received Ms. Fitzgerald's book proposal for *Canine Kitchen, Have Fun Making Easy and Nutritious Home-Cooked Meals for Your Dog.* Though the proposal is very interesting, I'm sorry to say that we have a very similar book in the works. We wish you luck with other publishers.

Thank you for your interest in BowTie™ Press.

Sincerely,

April Balotro
Editorial Assistant

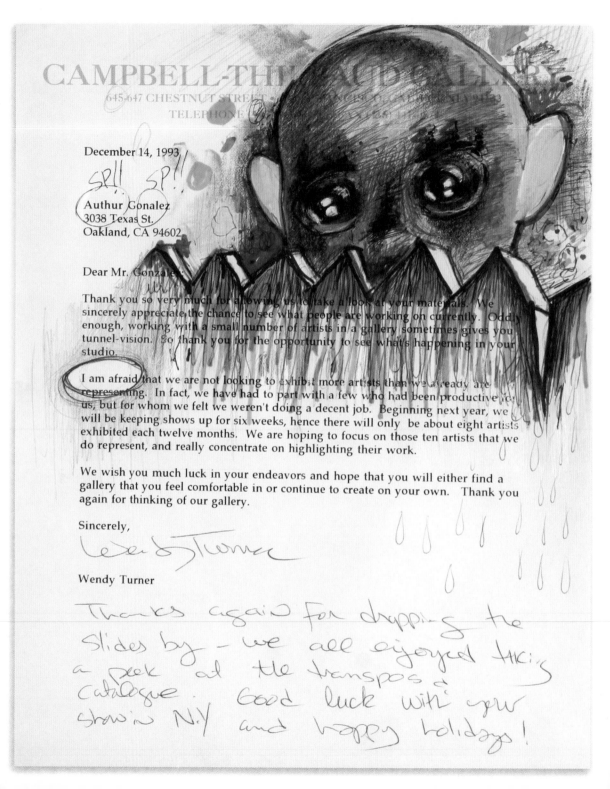

CAMPBELL-THIEBAUD GALLERY

645-647 CHESTNUT STREET · SAN FRANCISCO, CALIFORNIA 94133
TELEPHONE (415) 441-8680 · FAX (415) 441-8685

December 14, 1993

Authur Gonalez
3038 Texas St.
Oakland, CA 94602

Dear Mr. Gonzalez:

Thank you so very much for allowing us to take a look at your materials. We sincerely appreciate the chance to see what people are working on currently. Oddly enough, working with a small number of artists in a gallery sometimes gives you tunnel-vision. So thank you for the opportunity to see what's happening in your studio.

I am afraid that we are not looking to exhibit more artists than we already are representing. In fact, we have had to part with a few who had been productive for us, but for whom we felt we weren't doing a decent job. Beginning next year, we will be keeping shows up for six weeks, hence there will only be about eight artists exhibited each twelve months. We are hoping to focus on those ten artists that we do represent, and really concentrate on highlighting their work.

We wish you much luck in your endeavors and hope that you will either find a gallery that you feel comfortable in or continue to create on your own. Thank you again for thinking of our gallery.

Sincerely,

Wendy Turner

Thanks again for dropping the slides by — we all enjoyed taking a peek at the transpos & catalogue. Good luck with your show in N.Y and happy holidays!

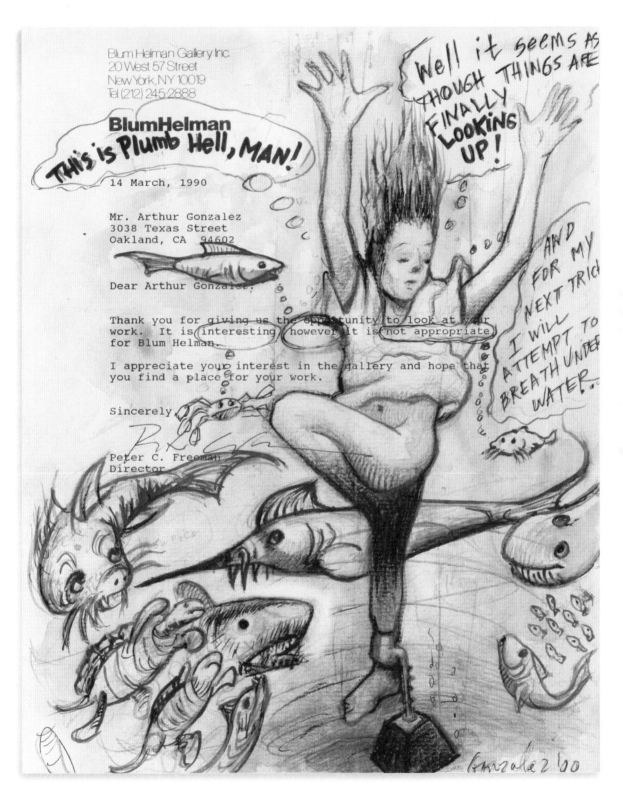

um, logistics seem pretty important to discuss, considering we're talking about a trip. and like I said, it concerns me that if I'm saying a conversation would help, that you'd continue to insist that one shouldn't be necessary.

your disinclination to accept, let alone acknowledge, thoughts and feelings I have that you don't want me to have or that you anticipate you might not like, is, to use your word, baffling. we're talking about you coming on a trip with my family, which would be a big deal even without the recent turbulence. (I had a vague sense of the dates and amount of time you said you wanted to go, but was thinking other ones would work better, so should I just give you the dates that work best for me without considering what's good for you? Why not figure it out together so it would work for both of us?)

I find your disinclination to engage with (or acknowledge the possible validity of) anything other than what it means for you in black and white terms difficult to understand. in other words, if you care about me enough to want to go on a trip with my family, why don't you care about me enough to be open to talking about what's on my mind, whether you deem it legitimate or not? and if you need to judge it, why do it before you even know what it is? maybe there's a reason for this that I'm not seeing, but short of an explanation from you, it's feeling like an impossible climate for a relationship.

I'm feeling like it's better if you don't come.

IN THE CIRCUIT COURT OF THE 11TH
JUDICIAL CIRCUIT IN AND FOR MIAMI-
DADE COUNTY, FLORIDA

FAMILY DIVISION

CASE NO. ȖƄ_76475FC16

IN RE: THE MARRIAGE OF   *

CYNTHIA A. RODRIGUEZ,   *

         Petitioner-Wife,   *

and   *   ***PETITION FOR DISSOLUTION
                                         OF MARRIAGE***

ALEXANDER E. RODRIGUEZ,   *

         Respondent-Husband.   *

      *

_____

      For her Petition for Dissolution of Marriage, the Wife states:

      1. **ACTION FOR DISSOLUTION:** This is an action for dissolution of marriage, which is being filed only after the Petitioner has exhausted every effort to salvage the marriage of the parties. However, "Alex" has emotionally abandoned his wife and children and has left her with no choice but to divorce him.

      2. **JURISDICTION:** The Court has jurisdiction over the parties and subject matter of this action.

      3. **RESIDENCY:** Both parties have been residents of the State of Florida for more than six months prior to the filing date of this petition.

      4. **MARRIAGE:** The parties were married to each other on November 2, 2002, in Dallas, Texas.

      5. **IRRETRIEVABLY BROKEN:** The marriage of the parties is irretrievably broken because of the Husband's extra marital affairs and other marital misconduct.

Maybe if you loved me a little bit-
more,
i wouldn't need to find it elsewhere
cheap distractions
imitations
of the real thing.
did i disapoint you that much,
that you cannot fully love me.
i see how you treat her
she is not beneath you,
but if she was,
that would make me too.. Right?
i'm stronger than that,
You will not hold me back,
with your looks of utter disdain.
disapointment etched into hard
sharp lines around your eyes.
i am a good person
an intelligent person
i have a future.
just you wait ~ see.

"Happy Fathers Day dad"

Draft

My dear Senator:

I read your telegram of February eleventh from Reno, Nevada with a great deal of interest and this is the first time in my experience, and I was ten years in the Senate, that I ever heard of a Senator trying to discredit his own Government before the world. You know that isn't done by honest public officials. Your telegram is not only not true and an insolent approach to a situation that should have been worked out between man and man but it shows conclusively that you are not even fit to have a hand in the operation of the Government of the United States.

I am very sure that the people of Wisconsin are extremely sorry that they are represented by a person who has as little sense of responsibility as you have.

Sincerely yours,

[HST]

IOWA STATE UNIVERSITY
OF SCIENCE AND TECHNOLOGY

March 17, 1998

College of Veterinary Medicine
Office of the Dean
2508 Veterinary Administration
Ames, Iowa 50011-1250
515 294-1242
FAX 515 294-8341

David ▓▓▓▓
6655 N Fresno St 213
Fresno, CA   93710

Dear David:

The Admissions Committee of the College of Veterinary Medicine has completed its review of applications for admission to the professional curriculum for fall 1998. The applicants' academic records have been carefully evaluated and given full consideration by the committee.

Admission to the College of Veterinary Medicine this year is more competitive than it has ever been, with over 1700 applicants for only 100 openings. As a result, there were many more qualified applicants than could be admitted to the professional curriculum.

We are sorry to advise you that you have not been accepted for admission to the College of Veterinary Medicine. If you wish to discuss the reasons we were unable to accept you into our professional curriculum, call 515-294-▓▓▓▓ to schedule a personal conference or a telephone conference with me.

Sincerely,

John H. Greve
Chair, Admissions
College of Veterinary Medicine

JHG/kk

From: Morgan, Victoria (NBC Universal) [mailto:░░░░░░░░░@nbcuni.com]
Sent: Tuesday, January 20, 2009 4:03 PM
To: Shannon Hogan
Subject: RE: Peta tape

The PETA spot submitted to Advertising Standards depicts a level of sexuality exceeding our standards. Listed below are the edits that need to be made. Before finalizing the spot, we would like to view a Quicktime file as well as a DVD . Thanks. Victoria Morgan

:12- :13- licking pumpkin

:13- :14- touching her breast with her hand while eating broccoli

:19- pumpkin from behind between legs

:21- rubbing pelvic region with pumpkin

:22- screwing herself with broccoli (fuzzy)

:23- asparagus on her lap appearing as if it is ready to be inserted into vagina

:26- licking eggplant

:26- rubbing asparagus on breast

Victoria Morgan
Vice President, Advertising Standards
NBC Universal
tel ░░░░░░░░░░
fax ░░░░░░░░░░

1-17-92

Dear Mama,
I'm sorry, I've tried
to change my aditude
but I can't help it

P.S. And I Know

you hate me

City of Cleveland
Legislative Department

July 12, 2007

Mr. Arsenio Winston
648 East 102 Street
Cleveland, Ohio 44108

Dear Mr. Winston:

As Councilman representing Cleveland's 11th Ward, I have been notified once again that you have been arrested for dealing drugs in my ward, this time at the Convenient Food Mart located at 18506 St Clair Avenue in the parking lot.

Mr. Winston, you have to be "dumber than mud." Don't you know that one of your so-called friends from the '8th-Avenue" gang ratted your stupid "ass" out that you were dealing drugs from the parking lot? They cut a deal. So much for your wonderful pals, you idiot. I am so glad that you are now 18 years of age, because now you are an adult and can no longer hide behind the juvenile court system, Mr. Quarterback, loser. Remember when you told me to "kiss your black ass" at R.J. Taylor Playground and that you were going to be an NFL Quarterback? Well, the NFL, despite perceptions, is "not for losers!"

In closing, I told you just recently to stay out of my neighborhood, you crack dealing piece of trash. Yet, you keep coming back because you think you are a big man. Well, real men go to school or to work every day and take care of their family, and not through illegal drug activity. You are a "thug" and you know what? There are only two places you will end up at the rate you are going – that is, prison or the nearest funeral home. Quite frankly, I don't care which one you get to first as long as your dumb stupid ass is out of my neighborhood.

Have a wonderful life, Arsenio. I am sure you have made your mother real proud. Remember when I spoke to her one of the other times that you were arrested for assaulting a police officer on East 185th Street? Only a moron would do that. Your fate is totally in your own hands; which, is a scary thought.

Go to jail or the cemetery soon,

Michael D. Polensek
Councilman, Ward 11

CC: Mr. Martin Flask, Director, Department of Public Safety
       Chief Michael McGrath, Chief of Police
       Commander Wayne Drummond, 6th District Police Headquarters
       Mr. Phillip Morris, *Plain Dealer*

Here is one of those dumb quotes that you hate, but I have in my room anyways: "Giving up does not always mean you are weak, sometimes it means you are strong enough to let go." I believe this is true, because it is exactly, word for word, how I feel about you. I'm trying desperately to forget my feelings about you, trying to bury them deep within my heart and let them dissipate. But it's difficult, because I have fallen so incredibly hard over you.

Basically, I am just crazy about you; everything you do/are, I admire, like, and adore. You've given me such incredible highs that I've quite literally become addicted to you. Every time I see you, right when you open my door, my heart stops a little because I get so excited. Every time I come into my room to find you sleeping, I feel like someone left me a little surprise. Every time you make me laugh, I realize how much I like you, want to be with you, and I feel like I have to hug you. And every time I see you sleeping, I want to marry you. (Wedding date: 9/21/2015).

But at the same time, my feelings and hopes are extremely and endlessly wrong and hopeless. What we've been doing is not normal and being the other girl isn't right. I'm sorry, but I just can't wait for you and it's led me to give up on the idea of us. Before Spring Break I tried to, but it only lasted for 15 minutes. Every time I tried giving up, I realized why I was in it to begin with: because of the way you make me feel and everything you do to me. But I'm trying to forget that because I realized that if someone truly did want to be with me, they wouldn't make me wait. I just feel like I deserve better than that. Maybe there is someone out there who will appreciate me in ways that you didn't. Despite all of my hopeful wishing, in the end, I guess we're not meant to be. It's an awfully terrible conclusion, I apologize.

I don't feel like myself. I guess what I'm trying to say is that I'm not proud of who I've been. I don't want to think of myself as the other girl, or have anyone else too for that matter. I feel guilty for everything I have done because it's not me. I promise. The person I usually am isn't this deceitful or self absorbed. I'm sorry for the person I've been and I'm sorry for poisoning everything. I like you, I do, and I can't ever deny that. But I humbly step aside and let nature take its course. "If you love someone, you set them free right?" in the words of the creeper. Hehe.

Ultimately, I'm just realizing how much one heart can take; I feel every happy and kind fiber of my body slowly unraveling. And, I can feel every infinitely small part of my aching heart deteriorating because of this, but I know and truly believe this is for the best. And, like you always say, "you'll get over it." And I will, I just need time.

p.s.: don't hate me.

INSIGHT

Box 7244, Grand Rapids, Michigan 49510

Dear *Sharon,*

A few days ago I received your manuscript and have now carefully
read and reviewed it. Although your story, poem or article is
well written and makes some excellent points, I am returning it
to you now for one of the following reasons:

- it's not appropriate for our teen-age audience
- it's too preachy
- it's too ordinary
- it's just not what I'm looking for at the moment

Since this is the first time you have ever submitted a manuscript
to our magazine, I suggest you carefully read the enclosed brochure
to make sure your manuscript is condusive to the style, purpose,
and audience of INSIGHT.

Thank you for considering INSIGHT. If you would like to examine an
issue of our magazine, feel free to ask. I'll be happy to send
you a free copy.

Sincerely,

Doris Rikkers

Doris Rikkers
Assistant Editor

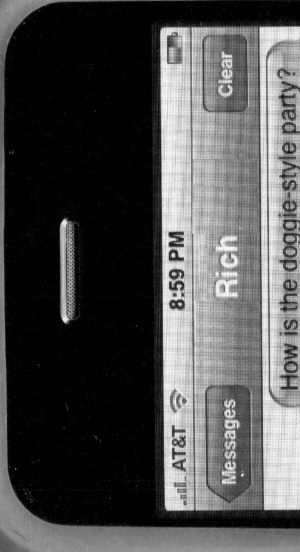

..ıl. AT&T 📶 8:59 PM 🔋

Messages **Rich** Clear

How is the doggie-style party?

Mar 7, 2009 10:14 PM

Im gonna get ready for bed. Hope it went well. Call me anytime in the night so i can hear your voice please.

I'm still awake. I am getting worried.

Mar 7, 2009 11:50 PM

Don't worried baby I'm fine Go sleep I'm talking drinking and I can't drive now but I'm almost sleeping kisses

Where are you sleeping?

Send

September 18, 2007

Nino Selimaj
Osso Buco
88 University Pl
New York, NY 10003

Dear Nino,

It has come to our attention that your restaurant, Osso Buco has displayed a picture of Chelsea Clinton in your front window. As you know, Ms. Clinton, a private citizen, was not consulted prior to this picture being displayed, and thus, her permission was not given for you to do so. While she may have dined at your restaurant, this does not serve as an endorsement.

Therefore, we ask that you immediately remove that picture and any and all pictures displaying Ms. Clinton. We reserve the right to exercise any and all options available to us if you refuse to comply.

Please confirm this understanding by written, return correspondence. We appreciate your cooperation.

Sincerely,

Douglas J. Band
Counselor to President Clinton

I'd work on your marketing. Do you really think telling me you have a "new project" is going to get me to view it? I don't even know who you are or what you do.

Remove me from your e-mail list please.

Mark Sorensen

----
hi.

i know you're not asking, but here's an unsolicited confession:
i am, as we touched on the first night, pretty fresh out of a long
relationship and i'm finding that i can't yet stomach dating. i reflexively
pull back like a nervous dog. i've had a great time with you and was instantly
attracted to you but i'm in this crappy anti-social head-in-the-sand phase
that i think is just going to take some time to shake off.

it's unfortunate because you're damn hot and a damn good boggler,
but...i just don't have it together right now.

oh, shit. yesterday was your birthday, wasn't it? happy birthday.

isn't this a great gift?!

WITH THE EXCEPTION OF ... WHO IS H-O-T, THE ENTIRE BOSTON RED SOX TEAM CAN GO FUCK THEMSELVES

BOSTON RED SOX 2007 BREAKS!

POOR IN MEDIOCRE YANKEES CHOKE!

SO, NEW YORK THREW BOSTON ONE TINY LITTLE!

WEST CHESTER AREA SCHOOL DISTRICT

Education Center • 829 Paoli Pike • West Chester, Pennsylvania 19380

November 21, 1986

Mr. and Mrs. ▓▓▓▓▓▓
▓▓▓▓▓▓▓▓ Lane
West Chester, PA 19380

Dear Mr. and Mrs. ▓▓▓▓▓,

On November 12, 1986, ▓▓▓▓▓▓▓▓▓ was evaluated for
placement in West Chester Area School District's gifted program.

At this time he/she has not met the requisites for gifted
program placement. This has been determined by a careful evaluation
of school records and test results, which I shall be happy to
review with you. You also have the right, following such a
conference, to a hearing to appeal the decision.

I have enclosed a letter from me to your child, for you
to use at your discretion. Please feel free to call me with
any questions or concerns at 436▓▓▓▓.

Sincerely,

Barbara R. Drizin
Supervisor, Gifted Program

BRD:nbl
Encl.
cc: Principal
       Counselor
       File

High Expectations PAY OFF

WEST CHESTER AREA SCHOOL DISTRICT

Education Center • 829 Paoli Pike • West Chester, Pennsylvania 19380

November 21, 1986

Dear _____ ,

    I want to thank you for talking to and working with a psychologist so that we could do a better job of teaching you in West Chester.

    As you know, people are different from each other in many ways. We have different physical appearances, ways of learning, likes, interests and needs. We try to give our students what they need in their educational program. Because you were considered for PROBE, we know you care about learning and are a successful student. You can be proud of that!

    We think that you will continue to do well in your present program—without PROBE. Perhaps in the future, PROBE will be a better program for your needs.

    Thank you for helping us learn more about you—and how best to teach you. I wish you continued success.

              Sincerely,

              Barbara R. Drizin
              Supervisor, Gifted Programs

BRD:nbl

High Expectations PAY OFF

From: MAILER-DAEMON@

Sent: Sat 2/15/2008

Subject: failure notice

<_____33@hc

71.74.56.243 doe

messagelabs.com
2:21 AM

mail.com>:
not like recipient.

July 7th, 1938

Dearest Scottie:

I don't think I will be writing letters many more
years and I wish you would read this letter twice -- bitter as
it may seem. You will reject it now, but at a later period
some of it may come back to you as truth. When I'm talking
to you, you think of me as an older person, an "authority,"
and when I speak of my own youth what I say becomes unreal to
you -- for the young can't believe in the youth of their
fathers. But perhaps this little bit will be understandable
if I put it in writing.

When I was your age I lived with a great dream. The
dream grew and I learned how to speak of it and make people
listen. Then the dream divided one day when I decided to marry
your mother after all, even though I knew she was spoiled and
~~meant what~~ meant no good to me. I was sorry immediately I
had married her, but being patient in those days, made the
best of it and got to love her in another way. You came along
and for a long time we made quite a lot of happiness out of
our lives. But I was a man divided -- she wanted me to work
too much for her and not enough for my dream. She realized
too late that work was dignity and the only dignity and tried
to atone for it by working herself but it was too late and she
broke and is broken forever.

It was too late also for me to recoup the damage --
I had spent most of my resources, spiritual and material, on
her, but I struggled on for five years till my health collapsed,
and all I cared about was drink and forgetting.

The mistake I made was in marrying her. We belonged
to different worlds -- she might have been happy with a kind simple man
in a southern garden. She didn't have the strength for the big stage --
sometimes she pretended, and pretended beautifully, but she didn't
have it. She was soft when she should have been hard, and hard when
she should have been yielding. She never knew how to use her
energy -- she's passed that failing on to you.

For a long time I hated her mother for giving her
nothing in the line of good habit -- nothing but "getting by"
and conceit. I never wanted to see again in this world women
who were brought up as idlers. And one of my chief desires in
life was to keep you from being that kind of person, one who
brings ruin to themselves and others. When you began to show
disturbing signs at about fourteen, I comforted myself with the
idea that you were too precocious socially and a strict school
would fix things. But sometimes I think that idlers seem to
be a special class for whom nothing can be planned, plead as one

will with them -- their only contribution to the human family is
to warm a seat at the common table.

My reforming days are over, and if you are that way I
don't want to change you. But I don't want to be upset by idlers
inside my family or out. I want my energies and my earnings for
people who talk my language.

I have begun to fear that you don't. You don't realize
that what I am doing here is the last tired effort of a man who
once did something finer and better. There is not enough energy,
or call it money, to carry anyone who is dead weight and I am
angry and resentful in my soul when I feel that I am doing this.
People like Rosalind and your mother must be carried because
their illness makes them useless. But it is a different story
that you have spent two years doing no useful work at all,
improving neither your body nor your mind, but only writing
reams and reams of dreary letters to dreary people, with no
possible object except obtaining invitations which you could
not accept. Those letters go on, even in your sleep, so that
I know your whole trip now is one long waiting for the post.
It is like an old gossip who cannot still her tongue.

You have reached the age when one is of interest to
an adult only insofar as one seems to have a future. The mind
of a little child is fascinating, for it looks on old things
with new eyes -- but at about twelve this changes. The adolescent
offers nothing, can do nothing, say nothing that the adult cannot
do better. Living with you in Baltimore -- (and you have told
Harold that I alternated between strictness and neglect, by which
I suppose you mean the times I was so inconsiderate as to have
T.B., or to retire into myself to write, for I had little social
life apart from you) -- represented a rather too domestic duty
forced on me by your mother's illness. But I endured your Top
Hats and Telephones until the day you snubbed me at dancing
school, less willingly after that. There began to be an un-
sympathetic side to you that alienated first Mrs. Owens, then
your teachers at Bryn Mawr. The line of those who felt it runs
pretty close to you -- adults who saw you every day. Among them
you have made scarcely a single close friend, with all your
mastery of the exterior arts of friendliness. All of them have
loved you, as I do, but all of them have had reservations, and
important ones: they have felt that something in you wasn't
willing to pull your weight, to do your part -- for more than
an hour.

This last year was a succession of information beginning
as far back as December that you were being unfair to me, more
frankly that you were cheating. The misinformation about your
standing in your class, the failure to tutor at the Obers at
Christmas, the unwillingness to help with your mother at Easter
in golf or tennis, then the dingy outbreak in the infirmary at
the people who were "on to you," who knew you had none of the
scholar in you but lived in a babyish dream -- of the dance favors
of a provincial school. Finally the catastrophe which, as far as
I am able to determine, had no effect except to scare you because

you knew I wouldn't maintain you in the East without some purpose
or reason.

If you did not have a charm and companionability, such
a blow might have chastened you, but like my Uncle Phil you will
always be able to find companions who will reassure you of your
importance even though your accomplishment is a goose-egg. To
the last day of his life Phil was a happy man, though he loafed
always and dissipated a quarter of a million of his own and his
sisters' money and left his wife in poverty and his son as you
saw him. He had charm -- great charm. He never liked me after
I was grown, because once he lost his charm in front of me and I
kicked his fat backside. Your charm must not have been in evidence
on the day Mrs. Perry Smith figuratively did the same to you.

All this was the long preparation for the dispair I
experienced ten days ago. That you did or did not know how I
felt about Baltimore, that you thought I'd approve of your meeting
a boy and driving back with him unchaperoned to New York by night,
that you honestly thought I would have permitted that -- well,
tell it to Harold, who seems to be more gullible.

The clerk from the Garden of Allah woke me up with the
telegram in which I mistook Simmons for Finney and I called the
Finneys -- to find them gone. The result was entirely a situation
of your own making -- if you had any real regret about the Walker
episode you'd have respected my wishes for a single week.

To sum up: what you have done to please me or make me
proud is practically negligible since the time you made yourself a
good diver at camp (and *now you are softer than you have ever been.*)
In your career as a "wild society girl", vintage of 1925, I'm not
interested. I don't want any of it -- it would bore me, like
dining with the Ritz Brothers. When I do not feel you are "going
somewhere", your company tends to depress me for the silly waste
and triviality involved. On the other hand, when occasionally
I see signs of life and intention in you, there is no company in
the world I prefer. For there is no doubt that you have something
in your belly, some real gusto for life -- a real dream of your
own -- and my idea was to wed it to something solid before it was
too late -- as it was too late for your mother to learn anything
when she got around to it. Once when you spoke French as a child
it was enchanting with your odd bits of knowledge -- now your
conversation is as commonplace as if you'd spent the last two
years in the Corn Hollow High School -- what you saw in Life and
read in Sexy Romances.

I shall come East in September to meet your boat -- but
this letter is a declaration that I am no longer interested in your
promissory notes but only in what I see. I love you always but
I am only interested by people who think and work as I do and it
isn't likely that I shall change at my age. Whether you will --
or want to -- remains to be seen.

Daddy

4

P. S. If you keep the diary, please don't let it be the dry
stuff I could buy in a ten-franc guide book. I'm not interested
in dates and places, even the Battle of New Orleans, unless you
have some unusual reaction to them. Don't try to be witty in the
writing, unless it's natural - just true and real.

P.P.S. Will you please read this letter a second time -- I wrote
it over twice.

Oakland
★★★★
All-America City
1993

CITY OF OAKLAND

LAKE MERRITT • 1520 LAKESIDE DRIVE • OAKLAND, CALIFORNIA 94612

Office of Parks and Recreation

(510) 238-3092
FAX: (510) 238-2224
TDD 839-6451

Cultural Arts Division
505-14th Street, Suite 715
Oakland, CA 94612

August 1, 1995

Arthur Gonzelez
Donna Billick
Studio 3088 Texas St.
Oakland, CA   94602

Dear Mr. Gonzelez:

On behalf of the Public Art Program of the City of Oakland, I would like to thank you for your recent submission of materials in consideration of the Montclair Village public art project. We appreciate your interest in the project and have enjoyed the opportunity of reviewing your work.

Unfortunately, you were not one of the artists selected to participate in the design proposal phase. The selection panel has chosen three artists whose aesthetics best represent the project parameters and objectives.

Thank you again for your interest in the Public Art Program. We wish you every success in your artistic endeavors.

Sincerely,

Rebecca Dube Ines
Public Art Program Assist

THE DAILY DIET OF RAW MEAT
SUCCESSES; REJECTIONS: Unfortunately, Although, Sorr

'07
Gonzalez

ZOLLA/LIEBERMAN GALLERY INC.

March 26, 1998

Arthur Gonzalez
1713 Versailles Ave.
Alameda, CA 94501

Dear Arthur,

Thank you for providing me with material in   ing me to your work. I am always
happy to acquaint myself with an artist's po   o. I found your work to be very
interesting.

Your work is strong however it is not in   dire   on of our gallery. Thank you for your
interest in Zolla/Lieberman Gallery.   wish y   he best of luck in finding appropriate
exhibition opportunities.

Sincerely,

Amy Wolff

Amy Wolff

AW/bf

JESSE E. ESCHBACH

JUDGE

January 19, 1965

Mr. James E. Bourne
1031 Hawthorne Drive
Bloomington, Indiana 47403

Dear Jim:

I sincerely appreciate your letter of January 12, 1965, and
I have enjoyed the opportunity of knowing you personally.
I am sure that with your record, you will make a success of
the practice of law.

I have now determined to make a commitment regarding my
clerkship and I have written the young man selected. This
is no reflection upon you or your ability, but I believe the
other young man has a higher interest in the experience
provided by a clerkship.

Again I want to commend you on the fine record you have made
in law school and extend to you my sincerest best wishes for
a prosperous and meaningful career in the law.

Sincerely yours,

Jesse E. Eschbach

JEE:vhg

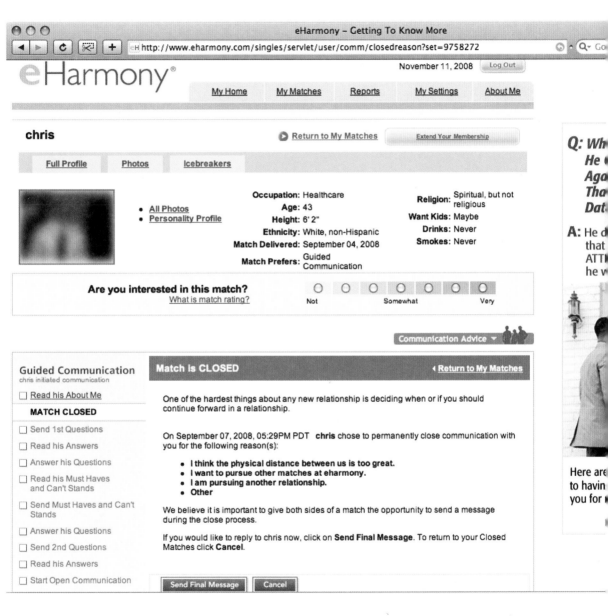

http://www.eharmony.com/singles/servlet/user/comm/closedreason?set=9758272

eHarmony®

November 11, 2008   Log Out

My Home   My Matches   Reports   My Settings   About Me

chris

▶ Return to My Matches   Extend Your Membership

Full Profile   Photos   Icebreakers

- All Photos
- Personality Profile

Occupation: Healthcare
Age: 43
Height: 6' 2"
Ethnicity: White, non-Hispanic
Match Delivered: September 04, 2008
Match Prefers: Guided Communication

Religion: Spiritual, but not religious
Want Kids: Maybe
Drinks: Never
Smokes: Never

Are you interested in this match?
What is match rating?

○ ○ ○ ○ ○ ○ ○
Not   Somewhat   Very

Communication Advice ▼

Guided Communication
chris initiated communication

☐ Read his About Me

MATCH CLOSED

☐ Send 1st Questions
☐ Read his Answers
☐ Answer his Questions
☐ Read his Must Haves and Can't Stands
☐ Send Must Haves and Can't Stands
☐ Answer his Questions
☐ Send 2nd Questions
☐ Read his Answers
☐ Start Open Communication

Match Is CLOSED   ◀ Return to My Matches

One of the hardest things about any new relationship is deciding when or if you should continue forward in a relationship.

On September 07, 2008, 05:29PM PDT **chris** chose to permanently close communication with you for the following reason(s):

- **I think the physical distance between us is too great.**
- **I want to pursue other matches at eharmony.**
- **I am pursuing another relationship.**
- **Other**

We believe it is important to give both sides of a match the opportunity to send a message during the close process.

If you would like to reply to chris now, click on **Send Final Message**. To return to your Closed Matches click **Cancel**.

Send Final Message   Cancel

Q: Wh
He
Aga
Tha
Dat

A: He d
that
ATT
he w

Here are
to havin
you for

From: ▨▨▨▨▨▨▨ <▨▨▨▨▨▨▨@gmail.com
Date: Mon, Apr 28, 2009 at 2:58 PM

i recently started seeing someone more regularly, and i wasn't really sure it was something i needed to tell you or not? i feel like we haven't really spent time together in weeks so it seemed sort of dot dot dot question mark about how or whether or not to announce new stuff. just thought maybe you'd like to know.

Dear Nutless Coward,

So you never wrote back to my letter. Klassy.

I don't care about your official "in a relationship" status, ok?
That is no goddamn excuse for not replying to me. I don't care
if you're in a stage where you're fucking everything that moves,
or you've started hanging out with someone, or you're
committed, or you're married with three kids, a minivan, and a
house in the suburbs. YOU FUCKING RESPOND. You man
the fuck up and face everything that comes your way, no matter
how uncomfortable it might be.

But really, no answer? More than a month later, and no answer
whatsoever. That's pathetic. I sent you the letter telling you
that I've been in love with you for seven years, but I'm the one
who thinks that you're pathetic. That's got to show you
something.

So you know what? Forget it. Don't worry about it. Just forget
I ever said anything to you. Erase my little message from your
inbox. I don't want you anymore.

Olivia

WELLS FARGO

Wells Fargo Business Direct
P.O. Box 29482
Phoenix, AZ 85038-8655
1-800-231-9244

September 19, 2008

Customer ID: 4260000███

Application for a *Wells Fargo*® Business Platinum card account

Dear David ███████

We are writing to you about your recent application for a *Wells Fargo* Business Platinum card account. Unfortunately, we are not able to approve your application at this time.

The decision was based on review of your credit application along with your business and personal credit histories which we obtained from the credit agency(s) listed below. Based on analysis of this information, we are unable to approve your application for the following reasons:

- Length of time since most recent personal credit bureau inquiry.
- Length of time business has been established.
- Number of inquiries within the last 6 months on consumer credit report.

By law, you are entitled to full disclosure, free of charge, of the information in your credit file by requesting a copy of your report from the agency(s) within 60 days. The agencies took no part in our decision **and are unable to provide the specific reasons why the adverse action was taken.** However, you have the right to dispute the accuracy and completeness of any information pertaining to you in your credit report provided by any agency by contacting the credit reporting agency(s) directly. You can contact the agency(s) directly at the phone numbers listed below to request a copy of the report.

Consumer Credit Agency
Equifax Customer Service
P.O. Box 740241
Atlanta, GA 30374
1-800-685-1111

If you have any questions about the information in this letter, please call us at 1-800-231-9244, Monday through Friday 7:30 a.m. to 5:00 p.m. Pacific Time. Any representative will be happy to assist you. If you prefer, you can write us at the address listed above.

We're sorry that we are unable to approve your application at this time. We offer a full range of products and services created exclusively for business owners like you and hope to be able to serve you in the future.

Respectfully,

mike Stratman

Very nice work but not
right for us.

Best of luck,

On 12/16/07, ~~███████~~ < ~~███████~~ @hotmail.com > wrote:

Hey ▬, Thanks so much for your patience over the last little while; I know that my schedule has been crazy and we haven't really been able to connect even though we have both wanted to.   It has given me a chance to think about everything though, which has been beneficial. One thing I have realized in the last few days is that you and I really seem to be looking for different things right now.   I know I haven't gotten into my "details" with you, but this is the first time since I was 16 years old that I've taken the opportunity to be single. Literally the night that we met while we were getting ready to go out, I told my girlfriends that I needed to be on my own for awhile. Obviously they died laughing after I launched myself through your cab window... which I'm sure I'll never live down. You are a very good catch and pretty irresistible and smart and funny and all of the really really juicy stuff – and this isn't a "just not into you" thing at all... it's really just a timing thing. I'm normally not like this, but I feel so selfish right now and I can't imagine treating you or anyone else the way you would deserve to be treated or the way that you treat me. To be fair, I think it's important that I take the chance to figure out some of my own stuff before I consider getting back into anything with anyone. Wow... I just read this over and it sounds horrible. I honestly do like you a lot and I want you to know that.   If you want to try starting over as friends, I'd be very happy. I do understand though if you would rather punch me in the face. And I wanted to tell you all of this in person today, so I'm very sorry for the e-mail.

Take care, S.

▬.

3-2172
8/7/52

UNITED STATES DEPARTMENT OF JUSTICE
Immigration and Naturalization Service
Ellis Island, New York Harbor 4, N.Y.

Please refer to
File No.

Dear Sir (Madam):

You are hereby informed it has been directed by the
Assistant Commissioner, Immigration and Naturalization Service,
Washington, D. C., that an order of deportation be not entered
at this time, but that you be required to depart from the
United States, without expense to the Government, within such
period of time and under such conditions as this office deems
appropriate.

In view of the foregoing, you should arrange to depart
from the United States on or before _____,
advising this office at least five days in advance of the date,
port and manner in which you intend to leave, so that your
departure may be verified by an officer of this Service and
your case closed.

You are further informed it was also directed in the event
you do not avail yourself of the privilege thus extended that
you be deported from the United States forthwith pursuant to
law.

Very truly yours,

EDW. J. SHAUGHNESSY
District Director
New York District

By:

PHILIP FORMAN, Acting Chief
Detention, Deportation and
Parole Branch

February 03, 1994

JENNIFER LYNN LUGOWSKI
FRESNO CA 93711

Dear JENNIFER LYNN LUGOWSKI:

The enclosed information pertains to your interest in immigrating to the United States of America. The information concerning your registration is noted at the end of the letter.

Unfortunately, visa numbers are not presently available for your use. You will be notified when further consideration can be given to processing your application for immigration. The reason for this delay is that there are more applicants for visas than there are immigrant visa numbers available under the limitation prescribed by law. For some visa categories, for example F3 or F4, this delay could be many years. Should you wish to know which priority dates are currently being processed, you may call the State Department's Visa Office at (202) 663-1541.

You are cautioned that you MUST NOT make any firm plans, such as disposing of property, giving up jobs, or making travel arrangements at this time. We have no way of predicting when it will be possible to proceed with your immigrant visa application.

You need not check with us further unless you need to report a change of address or a change in your personal situation which may affect your entitlement to an immigrant visa.

We will keep your case on file until further action is possible. When communicating with this office, either by telephone or letter, you must ALWAYS refer to your name and case number exactly as they appear below.

Case Number:	TRT – 19945060
PA Name:	LUGOWSKI, JENNIFER LYNN
Preference Category:	F2A SPOUSE OR CHILD (UNDER 21) OF LPR
Your priority date:	May 1993
Foreign State Chargeability:	CANADA

REMINDER: IT IS VERY IMPORTANT TO KEEP THIS OFFICE INFORMED OF YOUR CURRENT ADDRESS.

BACK TO THE BIBLE'S YOUTH MAGAZINE

Dear Teen:

    It's great to hear from you and to read some examples of your writing!
We're excited about your interest in the magazine as well as your desire
to express yourself creatively.

    We can't use your submission at this time, but don't let that discourage
you from trying again.

    Here are some suggestions that might help you better understand what
we're looking for: Poetry and first-person articles based on your own
experiences. We'd like to see you find a way of saying what's been said
a thousand times, using specific details to describe your thoughts and
feelings.

Thanks again, and keep it up.

Sincerely,

Lisa

Lisa Thompson
Associate Editor
TQ

BOX 82808 • LINCOLN, NE 68501 • (402) 474-4567

📖   Comcast   Translation   Facebook   Bulletin   P50 ▾   History ▾   math homework

facebook   **Home**   **Profile**   **Friends**   **Inbox**

| Inbox | Sent Messages | Notifications | Updates |

To: ▭ ✕

Subject: FB page for Mom

Message:

Hi Aunt ▭ ,

I forwarded you the old family pix that I have from you -- thank you so much for scanning those in the first place!

As for a public fb page, I wish I could participate in a project like that with more joy than pain, but 25 years later, I still can't. I love you sooooo much and am so happy and glad that Mom had you for a sister, and that you are celebrating her 65th birthday with something special.

I will definitely come look at the page when it is up, but please understand that I can't join a group for it, or join in on it. I just feel very private about losing her. I also don't feel strong enough to face the "pings" on my fb home page announcing that there has been another update or memory added. Losing mom was the worst experience of my life, and missing her is still my deepest pain. Daily life -- like Facebook -- is a place where I do not have to face that pain. I can't invite it in there, and I also can't mourn her death publicly again. It just hurts too much.

I am sure that the page WILL bring a lot of joy, and new memories, and much love. This fall I will pick a strong-feeling day and check it out in a way that I can predict and control, and I will love reading every bit of it. I hope that putting it together is a wonderful experience for you.

Much, much love,

▭

Attach: 🎥 Record Video   🔖 Post Link   👶 Add Childhood Memo...

🎁 Add Gift

Send   Cancel

🅕 Applications   🗃 👥 📅 📇 ◈ ◇   👤 ● Chat (Offline)

There is nothing to talk about.
Please stop contacting me.

July 5, 2006

Steve—

What happened to you? You were a kind, generous, honorable man. Now you've turned into this. angry, empty person. I can't even call you a man. anymore. You're not the man I fell in love with. This is not Steve ~~████~~ Steve ~~████~~ would never do these things. Steve ~~████~~ promised me he would never leave me and that he would never cheat on me; I believed him. You broke those promises. Steve ~~████~~ loved me deeply, and I know it was genuine. You ~~████~~ threw that all away and justified it to yourself by making things up about our relationship; problems tha never really existed. Steve ~~████~~ was proud of me for earning the money to go to Europe all by myself. You told people that you paid for my trip, when I wouldn allow ~~to~~ you to give me a dime. Steve ~~████~~ respect my money and my things. You cracked my rear bumpe on my car and messed up the airbag system, and didn't even mention it to me. You also charged someth to my debit card, when you never had permission to do such a thing.

Steve ~~████~~ was loyal, loving, & trustworthy. You cheated on me numerous times and ~~weren't~~ even man enough to tell me about it. You told me that she stayed in the guest room for just a few nights because ~~████~~ kicked her out and she couldn't afford her own place. You lied. You let her move into your bedroom (wh you used to call our room) after [redacted] found out about you two and kicked her out. And anyway, if she was so broke, how is it possible that she could afford a $116 plane ticket for you?

Steve [redacted] told me he would always tell me if something was wrong or if he needed space. You told me you were going to London.

Steve [redacted] would never yell at me. You yelled at me over the phone at work in front of everyone. Steve [redacted] loved me. You hate my guts for reasons that are all in your head. Steve [redacted] knew what a great relationship we had and knew how much I loved him. You won't even recognize that. Steve [redacted] would be there for me when I needed him. You were too busy on my birthday to even talk to me that night when I needed you after my car got broken into. You had better things to do on a Sunday afternoon than to comfort me over the phone when I was stuck in the Madrid airport all night.

Steve [redacted] showed me off to all his friends. You created a webpage that said you were single and demanded that I stay away from your friends. Steve [redacted] had alot of friends who respected him. You have lost the respect of many. Steve [redacted] loved his job and would do anything to achieve career success. You gambled on losing your job for a cliché.

I don't know what happened to Steve [redacted] To me, he

no longer exists. He was the love of my life; my forever. I do know that someday Steve ▓▓▓▓ will realize what he has done and deeply regret it. When that day comes, I will not be there. I never want to see or speak to you again.

I realize that you may never read this, but I can't have the last words said between us to be shouted out of anger over the phone.

I don't regret a second of our relationship because I know that I gave it my all. I gave my whole heart and soul to a man that I loved deeper than I have ever loved anyone before, and possibly deeper than I will ever love again; and that love was reciprocated. I will never have to blame myself for something I did or didn't do. I was honest, loyal, and trusting to a fault. I can hold my head up high and know that I did everything I could possibly do to make this relationship great. And it was great. You, on the other hand, do not have that priveledge. You have to carry this great guilt. The guilt that is actually weighing down your shoulders so much that you are slouching. Steve ▓▓▓▓ never slouched; he always stood up tall and proud because he had plenty of things in his life to be proud of. That was one of my favorite things about Steve ▓▓▓▓ You are so burdened by your mistakes that you actually look small and weak

You are not Steve ██████

I hope you find yourself and that you are happy. I ~~do~~ truly do. Have a nice life.

Brandee

The New York Times

229 WEST 43 STREET
NEW YORK, N.Y. 10036

ADAM MOSS
Editorial Director
The New York Times Magazine

February 8, 1996

Mr. Will Georgiades
Esquire
250 West 55th Street
New York, New York 10019

Dear Will,

Many thanks for your letter and story ideas. I'm afraid none work for us, however.

Probably the best contact for you here, if you have other ideas you want to pitch, is a very good story editor named Diane Cardwell. She handles entertainment. And do keep in mind, if you decide to come back to us, that our readership is a little more, well, staid, than you seem to think. "Asshole" is just never going to fly here.

Best,

February 14, 2009

KKM -

Based on your e-mail last fall, your
girlfriend now speaks for you. Here is
the antique amethyst ring that you
gave me in 1992 for our first
Christmas.

Good luck sharing your life with a
possessive woman who is obviously
threatened by a relationship that
ended well over a decade ago.

Please don't contact me again.

Eva

30 Day NOTICE OF TERMINATION OF TENANCY

CAUTION TO LANDLORD: Until 12-31-05 if the tenant has resided in the residential tenancy premises for one year or longer, you must give a 60 Day Notice of Termination of Tenancy rather than a 30 Day Notice of Termination of Tenancy. As of 1-1-05 you may give a 30 Day Notice of Termination of Tenancy unless your rental agreement states that a 60 day notice is required. (1) This "30 Day Notice of Termination of Tenancy" may only be used for month to month tenancies, for leasehold tenancies where the term of the lease has expired (tenancies "at will" or for tenancies with an unspecified term. It may NOT be used for leases or rental agreements that call for a specified date of termination which has not yet expired. (2) This Notice may be served concurrently with either a "3 Day Notice to Pay Rent or Quit" and/or a "3 Day Notice to Perform Covenant or Quit". It may not, however, be served concurrently with a "3 Day Notice to Quit". (3) Use of this "30 Day Notice of Termination of Tenancy" may not be appropriate in counties where specific rent control ordinances are in effect where your written Rental Agreement or Lease, if any, provides for a longer period than thirty days notice, or specifically provides for additional or specific language to be contained in a "Notice of Termination of Tenancy". If you are uncertain as to the specific requirements to apply to your own circumstances, you should consult with an attorney who specializes in landlord/tenant law. (4) This Notice need not be given at the beginning of the month or the beginning of the rental period, but may be given at any time during the month, rent will be prorated accordingly. Again, prior to using this form, please consult with your landlord-tenant attorney.

TO: _____

AND ALL OTHER OCCUPANTS, TENANTS, AND SUBTENANTS IN POSSESSION OF THE TENANCY PREMISES
[Cannot to landlord. Save the names of ALL known ADULT occupants in possession of the premises, whether they are named in the Rental Agreement or not, whether they contracted with the Landlord or not, and whether they are in possession of the tenancy premises with permission of the Landlord or not]

PROPERTY ADDRESS: _____ SILVERWOOD RD. W. SACRAMENTO 95691

NOTICE IS HEREBY GIVEN that pursuant to California law, your occupancy and tenancy of the above-described tenancy premises is terminated as of THIRTY days from the date stated below. You are hereby required to deliver up possession of said tenancy premises to the Owner, Landlord, or his/her Authorized Agent not later than 30 days from the date of service of this notice.

Your failure to comply with the foregoing will result in legal proceedings being instituted against you to recover possession of said premises for UNLAWFUL DETAINER. Also, such proceedings could result in a judgment against you for unpaid rent, costs of suit, necessary disbursements, damages, attorneys fees (if you have a signed, written rental agreement allowing for attorneys fees) as well as statutory damages for such unlawful detention, and to declare a forfeiture of the lease or rental agreement, if any, under which you occupy the above-described tenancy premises.

YOU ARE STILL RESPONSIBLE FOR THE DAILY PRO-RATED RENT THAT BECOMES DUE THROUGH THE EXPIRATION DATE OF THIS "*30 Day Notice of Termination of Tenancy.*" [This notice is not an attempt to collect a debt]

DATED: _____ 4-18-08 _____

_____
Signature of landlord, property manager, etc.

PENAL CODE SECTION 594 STATES THAT "EVERY PERSON WHO MALICIOUSLY INJURES OR DESTROYS ANY REAL OR PERSONAL PROPERTY NOT HIS OWN...IS GUILTY OF A MISDEMEANOR."

Notice to Occupants: As required by law, you are hereby notified that a negative credit report reflecting on your credit history may be submitted to a credit reporting agency if you fail to fulfill the terms of your credit obligations. Under no circumstances will this *Thirty Day Notice of Termination of Tenancy* be waived, canceled, discharged, revoked, rescinded, invalidated, or withdrawn without a signed, written document from the landlord expressly and specifically stating that this *Thirty Day Notice of Termination of Tenancy* notice is either waived, canceled, discharged, revoked, rescinded or withdrawn. No verbal promise, statement, representation or conduct by landlord, owner, or the authorized agent of either, will be considered as a waiver, cancellation, discharge, revocation, rescission, invalidation, or withdrawal of this *Thirty Day Notice of Termination of Tenancy* with which you are being served.

You are herewith also notified that you have the right to request an initial inspection of your unit and be present during the inspection. The purpose of this inspection is to allow you the opportunity to correct any deficiencies in the unit, before the termination date identified in this notice, in a manner consistent with the rights and obligations of the parties under the rental agreement in order to avoid deductions from the security deposit, if any, for reasonable and necessary cleaning to return the residential tenancy premises to the same level of cleanliness it was in at the inception of the tenancy and/or for reasonable and necessary repair of damages exclusive of ordinary wear and tear caused by the tenant or by a guest or licensee of the tenant. Contact the Landlord or Authorized Agent for the landlord to request an initial inspection. If you do not make such a request, there will be no duty on the part of the landlord or agent to conduct a Pre-Termination Inspection. The inclusion of this paragraph is not to be construed by you as an acknowledgment or admission that you have in fact paid a security deposit to the landlord.

IF a "3 Day Notice to Pay Rent or Quit" is served concurrently herewith, mere payment of the "Amount Due" will not negate this "Thirty Day Notice of Termination of Tenancy", you must still vacate possession of the tenancy premises not later than the expiration date of the thirty day period specified herein. IF a "3 Day Notice to Perform Covenant(s) or Quit" is served concurrently herewith, you must also perform the covenant(s) specified therein; however, mere performance of the covenant(s) will not negate either this "30 Day Notice of Termination of Tenancy" or the "3 Day Notice to Pay Rent or Quit". In other words if you fail to comply with the demand of any three day notice issued to you, a lawsuit for Unlawful Detainer can be filed against you immediately after the 3 day period.

PROOF OF SERVICE

This portion is not to be completed by the "Server" until AFTER the service is completed!

CAUTION TO SERVER: Each and every ADULT occupant in possession of the premises (whether named on the rental agreement or not, whether they are in possession with permission of the Landlord or not, whether they contracted with the Landlord or not), should be served by at least one of the following methods: (Note that method (2) may be used only if method (1) is unsuccessful, method (3) may be used only if methods (1) and (2) were tried, but were unsuccessful) Method (4) is also permissible.

On (Date): _____ 4-18-08 _____ I, the "Server" served this "*30 Day Notice of Termination of Tenancy*" as follows:
Check One

☐ **PERSONAL DELIVERY:** I personally handed a copy of this "*30 Day Notice of Termination of Tenancy*" to these ADULT occupants/tenants:

☐ **SUBSTITUTED SERVICE:** I personally handed a copy of this "Notice to Vacate" to a person of suitable age and discretion (other than the above-named occupants(s), at the occupant(s) place of residence or employment AND mailed a copy to each ADULT occupant by first class mail, postage prepaid to the tenancy address stated above.

☒ **POSTING & MAILING:** Inasmuch as none of the occupant(s) have a separate place of employment, nor is it known to me, and no person of suitable age and discretion could be found at the place of employment, if any, or the tenancy address, I affixed a copy of this Notice to Vacate in a conspicuous place at the tenancy address AND mailed a copy to said tenancy address to each ADULT occupant by first class mail, postage prepaid.

☐ **CERTIFIED OR REGISTERED MAILING:** I mailed a copy of this Notice to Vacate to the tenancy address to ALL the ADULT occupants by registered or certified mail, postage prepaid.

AT THE TIME OF THE SERVICE I WAS AT LEAST 18 YEARS OF AGE. I DECLARE UNDER PENALTY OF PERJURY UNDER THE LAWS OF THE STATE OF CALIFORNIA THAT THE FOREGOING IS TRUE AND CORRECT, AND THAT IF CALLED AS A WITNESS I COULD DO SO COMPETENTLY. THIS DECLARATION WAS EXECUTED ON THE BELOW STATED DATE AT (City) _West Sacramento_, CALIFORNIA.

DATED: _____ 4-20-08 _____ Signature of server _____

This notice is not intended as legal advice. For proper preparation of this notice you should consult with an attorney familiar with landlord-tenant laws. No liability is assumed for improper preparation or use.

THIS FORM IS PROVIDED AS A COURTESY OF THE LAW OFFICE OF GARY LINK, Sacramento, CA (916) 447-8101
Copyright; Law Office of Gary Link, October, 2005

Date: October 9, 2008 8:28:13 AM PDT
Subject: RE: from eharmony

Hey B,

At the moment I'm not up for the long drive thing or should I say, more honestly, there are other eharmony opportunities that are a lot closer.

H

Rosellen Brown • **General Delivery, Peterborough, NH 03458** •

Phone / FAX 603

June 25, 1996

Dear ███████████████

Bad enough that I'm going to up-end your optimistic approach to the impossible in your life, but first I have to apologize for the fact that your letter to me -- the envelope says March! -- has bounced around quite inefficiently from my home in Houston to Chicago where we've spent the year and finally to New Hampshire, my ex-home, to which we return each summer. Even with all those destinations it shouldn't have taken as long as it did -- I suspect some inefficient tenants at the Houston end who have bungled more than one postal caper over the course of the year. Apologies.

But to cut to the chase. I appreciate your being a fan, and I certainly do respect and envy your buoyant approach to the unlikely, but unfortunately, having said that, I have to add that one more request for a few words for a book jacket is going to drive me to suicide -- and I'm not exaggerating much, believe me. **Some day -- could be any day now -- when** my star has fallen and nobody cares to have my name appended to their work, I might be nostalgic for the seasons in which I was in demand as a recommender. But for the moment I have the feeling that if I wanted to I could spend all my time doing blurbs and none writing anything of my own and people might wonder whatever became of me...present on so many covers but never again on my own, how odd.

Which is to say that I'm really sorry, but I just can't do another one. Please don't think me churlish but the best I can do is wish you much luck with your collection, and hope you can find some faster readers, or perhaps a few who don't bother to read the work in question at all (there are such), though they very well might be missing out on a good book. I might be too, with apologies to its author.

Very best,

Rosellen Brown

I love you.

More than I've been able to express, but not enough for you to be happy with me.

I love you.

I want to spend the rest of my life with you, but not with you treating me like this.

I love you.

Please know that I never have, don't right now, and never will love anyone else.

I love you.

I'm addicted to your touch, in every way that it moves me, in every place that you choose to caress...

I love you.

But for all the wrong reasons.

I love your love, I love your touch...and both of those are gone right now.

I love you.

Because you are different.

But now I see that I've loved you for the things you were NOT, instead of who you are.

I have put up with them because "nobody's perfect" and because "you put up with me first" and because "it'll get better as soon as he sees that it's ok, that nothing's wrong..."

But they aren't going away. They are growing bigger and stronger and showing up faster and longer...

I love you.

But I refuse to let you take this place from me.

I love you.

But I want to have guy *friends*.

I love you.

But I believe in myself now. More than you do.

I love you.

And you were right; I will be just fine without you.

APPLICATION FOR EXECUTIVE CLEMENCY

Frank Merriam

To His Excellency, ~~JAMES ROLPH, *Jr.~~, *Governor of California:*

SIR: I hereby make application for __commutation of sentence__

from the __California State Prison__ at __San Quinten, California,__

and respectfully represent as follows:

Name __Jose Aragon__ ; Prison No. ; Age ;

Nationality __Mexican__ ; County where convicted __Riverside.__ ;

Crime __Murder__ ; Date of sentence ;

Term of sentence __Death__ ; Sentence expires __Execution July 13th, 1934;__ ;

Name of Judge __O. K. Morton__ ; of Prosecuting Attorney __Earl Redwine__ ;

Did you plead guilty? __No__ ; Did you have a jury trial? __Yes__ ;

Are you now in prison? __Yes__ ; If paroled, when? __No__ ;

Have you applied for parole? __No__

Name and address of Attorney who defended. *(Whether retained by defendant or appointed by the Court)—*
__C. W. Benshoof, Riverside, California.   Appointed by Court__
__Wallace Rouse, Indio, California.   Appointed by Court.__

If case appealed to Supreme Court, give its number or other designation
__NO.__

Were you ever before convicted of any crime? __No__ ; If so, state when, where, and what for

What was your former trade or occupation? __Laborer__

__N. Nasato__

Are you married? _____ No, widower. _____ ; If so, give name and place of residence of your husband or wife _____

Have you any children or other relatives dependent upon you for support? _____ Yes. _____

If so, state name, age and place of residence _____ Josephene Aragon, age 4, Indio, California.
Francisco, and Barbara Aragon, aged 3 years and Barbara 11 months, both
at Indio California. _____
Were you living with and supporting your family at the time of your conviction? _____ Yes

If not, state reason _____

Have you ever made previous application for executive clemency? _____ I have not. _____

If so, what decision was rendered? _____

Attach hereto a short statement setting out reasons why you believe executive clemency should be granted you.

Pasqual Torres had been out with my wife three different nights late without
my consent. Just before I killed them I heard Pasqual tell my wife to be
ready and he would be after that evening. At noon I told my wife not to go
on account of our children, she said she would go with Pasqual. Then I
talked to Pasqual about it and he said he was going to take my wife away
that evening. I tried to get him not to, but he said he would. Then he
stooped to get piece iron pipe but I picked one other piece of pipe and
killed him. I turned around and my wife was coming she said to protect
Pasqual, I was so mad I was crazy, and I could not bear to see her go.
killed her to.

Subscribed and sworn to before me, this _____ 3rd _____ day of _____ July _____ 19 34

Jose Aragon

Winton Murphy
Notary Public in and for the County of
Marin, State of California
My Commission Expires Sept. 3, 1934

OFFICE OF THE WARDEN

CALIFORNIA STATE PRISON
AT SAN QUENTIN

PLEASE REFER TO
FILE NO. 55984 Exe.Data

July 13, 1934.

Hon. Frank F. Merriam,
Governor of California,
Sacramento, California.

Dear Sir:

In accordance with the law, and the judgment of the
Superior Court in and for the County of Riverside, State

was executed within the walls of this prison today,

July 13th., 1934, at 10:13½ o'clock in the forenoon.

Respectfully,

[signature]

Warden.

JBH:K.

I've given a lot of thought to what I want to say here. I've waited a couple of days until the emotions I felt upon reading your letter subsided. I write this with a clear head, sure of every word and nuance.

I appreciate that you took the time to call the alumni association, then Jianna, then my parents, in order to track down my address. Kinda dramatic though, don't you think? I mean, you could have found me on facebook in two seconds. But I know this isn't really about what you went through to find me—it's about you *telling* me what you went through to find me. Like I'm supposed to be impressed.

You know what's funny? Wait, let me rephrase that: You know what's sad? You spent half your letter describing the lengths you went to to find me after all of these years but you never explained why you bothered. Saying "it's been a long time" doesn't begin to count as an explanation (which I did not expect) for what you did. Nor does it count as an apology (which I did expect). Do you even remember why I stopped talking to you? Just because it happened a long time ago doesn't put what you did to me in soft-focus. Obviously, I have not gotten over it.

Part of friendship is trust, and I know that I will never be able to trust you. I have many, many wonderful friends in my life and I do not need any who I need to wonder about.

Bye.

August 10, 1969

To the Editor
Arizona Daily Star
Tucson

Dear Sir:

A friend recently sent me a clipping from   *yr alleged*
your newspaper. It's an editorial aptly
entitled "Baloney" from your June 29th
issue, ~~was~~ in which you seem to accuse
both Wallace Stegner and myself of writing
about the West without adequate knowledge
of the region. But on this point Wallace
Stegner requires no defense, as anyone even
slightly acquainted with his career should
know; and for myself, though I have lived
only twenty-two years in the Southwest (so
far) I am willing to bet my ~~dxxx~~ bottom
dollar that I have seen at least as much
of it as the writer of your editorial.

When I wrote in my review of Stegner's book
that "there is no West anymore" I meant
the West as a distinct <u>cultural</u> region.
Of course our unique landscape still remains
(or those portions of it which have not
yet been flooded by ~~thxxxxxxxxxxxx~~ dams,
disemboweled by ~~the~~ copper mines, buried
under asphalt and obscured by fungus-bearing
smog) but the general way of life, as typified
by our overgrown cities, is ~~pxttxxxxxxx~~
patterned after that of Los Angeles. Can
you deny it?

You claim the Old West ~~txxxxxxxxxxxxxxxx~~
still exists in much of its "primitiveness
and squalor" (your words). Here I agree with
you; it still exists, all right, in the
primitive minds and squalid greed of those
promoters and expansionists whose highest
ambition appears to be the debasement of Arizona,
New Mexico and Utah to the level of southern
California's ant-hill existence.

Edward Abbey
North Rim
Arizona 86022

From: Elizabeth Larock
Sent: Thursday, June 19, 2008 10:46 AM
To: Davida Kales
Subject: rejection

Hi sweetie. Sadly, I don't think I have any rejection letters. I think the last time I received them I was applying to colleges and I don't think I saved any of those. Your offer has really prompted me to take a closer look at my life, though. I don't have any rejection letters in my possession and it's not because I always have excelled at everything I've done, I think it's because I haven't put myself out there enough - haven't taken enough chances. I've always taken the safe route and haven't left myself any room for failure. It'd be so interesting to see who has the most rejection letters and to see how successful that person is. I would be willing to bet that those people who put themselves out there the most (and subsequently get rejected a lot) are the ones who have achieved the most career success. I'm completely inspired by your project and have decided to start collecting rejection letters (i.e. I'm going to start putting myself out there a whole lot more without the fear of rejection). When is your deadline for submission? Hope all is well.   xoxo Lizzie

Lizzie Larock
Owner, Old Town Pub & Restaurant
P.O. Box 882050
Steamboat Springs, CO 80487
970-879-2101
www.theoldtownpub.com
Not Your Usual Pub Grub (you'll love it!)

Brooke Alexander, Inc
59 Wooster Street, NY, NY 10012
212-925-4338

26 May 1990

Arthur Gonzalez
3038 Texas Street
Oakland, CA 94602

Dear Arthur Gonzalez:

Enclosed are the materials you sent to the gallery. They have been reviewed and are enclosed herewith.

Sincerely,

Brooke Alexander

Dear Mom,

I've run away. No telling
where I might go.
Well good-bye forever!
I'm—

Claire

P.S. I'm glad I'm leaving toward Claud

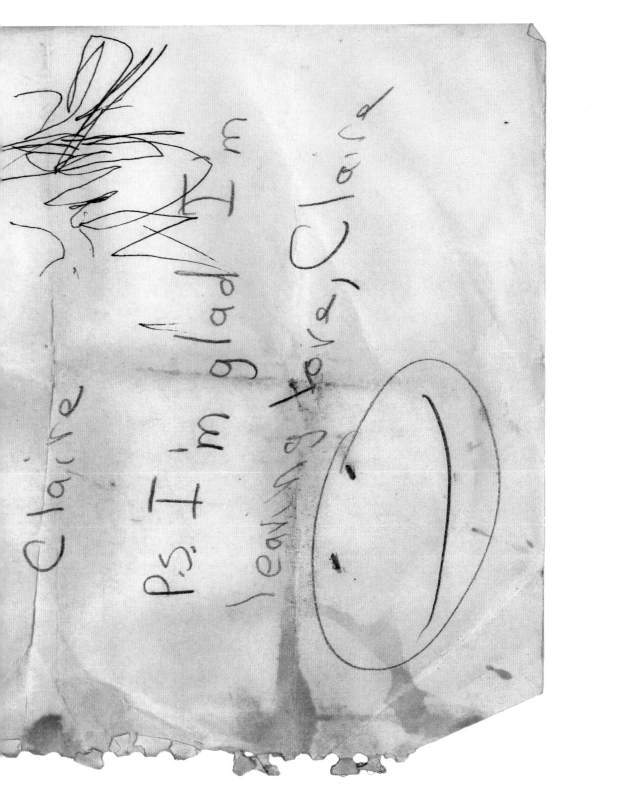

POSTSCRIPT

What happened after the rejection?
Here's the story behind a few of the letters and an update on how some of the recipients have fared.

Your letter of recent date has been received in the Inking and Painting Department for reply

In **1937**, Walt Disney awed audiences with *Snow White and the Seven Dwarfs*, the world's first full-length animated feature. A few months later, Mary Ford, a young art-school grad from Searcy, Arkansas, applied to work at Disney Studios. When she came up against Disney's then-restrictive hiring policy, Mary veered toward a career teaching middle-school art. But she kept this letter in a box for sixty-five years, bringing it out only occasionally. Upon Mary's death in 2003, her family had it framed.

We appreciate your interest in the Marine Corps

Bill Dobrow was twelve years old when he decided to join the Marines. The Corps politely declined, encouraging him to get his high-school diploma before enlisting. Not long after he received this letter, Bill, who'd been messing around on the drums for a couple of years, formed his first band. Bill let the Marines go, but he stuck with the drums; in recent years, he has recorded and toured with the Black Crowes, Sean Lennon, and Martha Wainwright, among others.

Reduction of large breast

Roslyn applied to her insurance company for a breast reduction and was denied. She switched insurers and tried again. Same story. Her third insurer approved the procedure, and at press time, the operation was scheduled.

We have been through this again and again

The letter was written twelve years ago. It was never sent.

Dear Mr. Gonzalez: Thank you for sending me the enclosed materials

Tired of receiving thanks-but-no-thanks form letters from galleries, NEA grantee

Arthur Gonzalez turned the tables. His Art of Rejection collection, pages of which are featured throughout this book, portrays dozens of his responses to years of rebuffs. (It is available at artgiftnet.com.) Today, the California College of the Arts professor uses his series to teach students about the art of hard work and the value of sly humor.

Notice of Default

It was December 2005, the height of the real-estate boom. A California couple bought a second home with plans to flip it for a nice profit. But six months later, the housing market buckled, and when their tenant was unable to pay her rent, the couple couldn't make their mortgage payments. With this letter, they walked away from the investment, incurring $50,000 in debt and severe damage to their credit rating.

You are very stubborn but you are mine

Celebrated photographer Bill Owens received this dressing-down from his mother when he was ten years old. He doesn't remember what he did to deserve the note, but he has saved it for sixty years.

Re: Childcare Biting Incidents

Whether the child learned her lesson from the suspension or simply outgrew the desire to bite other children, it is impossible to say. Either way, she returned to the Peak Performance day-care facility more than a year ago; the owner describes her recent behavior as "exemplary."

I'm not really sure why you're contacting me

Theirs was a long-distance relationship. He talked frequently about her moving back to L.A. . . . and he looked at condos they could live in together. . . and he even mentioned marriage. But when she told him she was seriously considering leaving New York and coming west, he broke off the relationship, saying only, "There's something missing." She later learned that this throw-away-my-keys e-mail so scared him that he was afraid to call her when he ended up moving to New York for work a few months later.

Thank you for your interest in The Putnam Publishing Group

Matthew Martin was a young law-school grad and although many of his peers were bound for high-paying jobs at big firms, his heart was set on book publishing. In the end, the lawyer who turned Matthew away in this letter not only hired him three months later but became instrumental in guiding his career. And, then, of course, there's the hand-written note from Matthew's father at the bottom of the page: "Matt—sounds encouraging." Dad was right.

I. Water Frog Certificate . . . .

Five-year-old Julie simply could not master the face float—as these certificates clearly attest. But a decade later, her strong freestyle—and, no doubt, face-float skills—earned her the **1989** and **1990** girls' swim-team MVP title at Piner High School in Santa Rosa, California.

Hi Michael, I hope you survived the holidays

Michael Hearst, half of the lit-rock band One Ring Zero, sent an e-mail to Michael Chabon (author of the Pulitzer Prize-winning novel *The Amazing Adventures of Kavalier & Clay*), asking if he would contribute lyrics to an album Hearst was recording. Chabon turned him down . . . but One Ring Zero spun the rejection into a catchy tune. At the bottom of Chabon's e-mail, you can see where, chord by chord, Hearst began scratching out the song he eventually titled "MC." (Listen to it on YouTube; search "One Ring Zero MC".)

Thank you for your recent letter and interest in the Giants

At thirteen, Danny Brown was already a huge Giants fan. He collected their baseball cards, knew their stats, and was sure the last-place Giants could win the **1984** World Series if only they would listen to his advice. So he wrote to the owner, recommending himself as the team's new manager. Today, Brown is a sports reporter for the *San Jose Mercury News* and, yes, he has covered the Giants.

Dear Jed, I assume that since I have not heard from you I'm not a priority in your life

August 27, 1997

Dear Jed,

I assume that since I haven't heard from you I'm not a priority in your life. This makes me angry and sad but I think it's the right thing for both of us. I can't do this any longer. The experience of being with you occasionally isn't worth the frustration and upset I feel from it. You've been telling me all along that you don't have the ability to be involved in a relationship but enjoy my company from time to time. You also said that I needed to decide when I'd had enough of our "casual arrangement". I've been listening but not really getting the message until now. Somehow, your life swallows you up so that you can't let anybody in close. Personally, I think you are missing out on a great opportunity with me, but of course I have a bias.

Eva and Jed had been seeing each for about a year. Despite her strong physical connection to him, Eva knew she wanted more than the casual encounters that suited his style. With this note, she called things off to free her life for something more permanent. Within a year she met Terry, who never went home after their second date. They've been married for nearly eight years.

Subject: Request for Discharge

After serving less than a year in the military—and shortly after this paperwork was filed—Private James Hendrix was discharged. He later became a professional guitarist and changed his name to Jimi.

Joyce, Paul told me about your talk last night

Meg and Joyce had been friends for three years; they'd met when their boys played T-ball together. Although Meg was single and Joyce married, their friendship worked. Eventually, though, Joyce and her husband, Paul, split up; within a year, Joyce had moved in with someone new and the friendship between the women waned. Paul began to talk to Meg at their kids' baseball games, and then asked her out. Since Joyce was happily settled with her new boyfriend, Meg assumed that she wouldn't mind if she and Paul went on a date. She was wrong. This goodbye letter was Meg's attempt to explain her painful decision to choose a new opportunity over an old friend. The women have not spoken since the day Meg gave this letter to Joyce.

Anthony, thanks for the book

Photographer Tony Stamolis has received his fair share of "no-thanks" notes much like this one. But in 2008, he got the yes he was waiting for: A publisher agreed to print his first book, *Frezno*, a dark and dramatic homage to his California hometown.

I am afraid that I have never been a very useful member of the Daughters of the American Revolution

With this typed letter, First Lady Eleanor Roosevelt resigned from the Daughters of the American Revolution after the group refused to let African American singer Marian Anderson perform at its Washington DC concert hall. The first lady and the president found a more suitable venue for Anderson: On Easter Sunday, 1939, the contralto sang on the steps of the Lincoln Memorial before a crowd of 75,000.

I just cant do it

> I just cant do it. I believe that you want to be with me now, but I don't believe that you will in three months, or even one. You know it breaks my heart, because there is nothing more that ive wanted than to be with you since may ... but ▬▬ i am wrung dry. i am worn out ... im tired, and i still feel broken. and i want to hit you and throw things at you and scream that you're an idiot for not seeing me for who i am sooner ...

They met while tending bar at the same college-guy watering hole. She had just come out of a three-year relationship. He hadn't been in a relationship for years. Things went well at first, but then came his drunken admission, her deep disappointment, a fair amount of yelling, and back-and-forth arguing that lasted for months. In the end, he moved out of town—only to leave her messages saying he wished she would take him back. This note was her response.

Dear Clay: Thank you for applying for the Astronaut Candidate Program

This letter represents the fifteenth time NASA turned away Clay Anderson from its astronaut training program. And yet the note gave Clay hope: Most applicants receive postcards; a letter sent on stationery meant something. The then twenty-nine-year-old aerospace engineer and his wife agreed he would apply one last time, and in 1998, on his sixteenth attempt, Clay was selected to join the program. Since then he has lived on the International Space Station and explored the ocean depths through NASA's Neemo Project. You can read his expedition journals at www.nasa.gov (enter "Journals Anderson" in the search field).

Thank you for your interest in the CST Division

This nondescript letterhead belongs to the CIA's Clandestine Service Trainee program, gateway for aspiring American spies. The applicant landed an interview with the CIA, but was told he needed more international experience. The clock is ticking: At twenty-eight, he has seven years to beef up his global credentials before hitting the agency's age limit for new recruits. He holds on to this letter to keep him focused on the world he someday hopes to join.

Dear Author

Zoe Gayl moved to New Mexico when she was fifty-seven and three-quarters, started performing stand-up comedy at sixty-one, and finished her roman à clef, *Three Lives and Then Some,* two years ago, at seventy-three. Since then, she has received sixty-four rejection letters, a few of which are collected here. She remains hopeful.

Dear Doofus Kendle

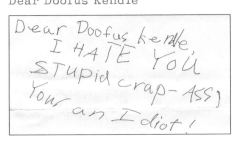

Alex wrote this missive to Kendall after she purposefully popped his favorite balloon. They were both eight at the time.

Dear Brother Hardy

Disenchanted Mormon Chad Hardy was fed up with religious intolerance, both in and out of his church. By publishing "Men on a Mission," a calendar he created featuring his Mormon brethren—shirtless— he knew he would test the Church's limits.

He was right: The Church of Jesus Christ of Latter-Day Saints responded not only by withholding Hardy's recently earned Brigham Young University degree but by excommunicating him. Although Hardy's calendar enterprise (viewable at www.mormonsexposed.com) has been a success, the excommunication caused deep pain for him and his family, who believe he will not be with them in the afterlife.

As we have discussed in today's meeting, your position is being eliminated effective February 2, 2009

She had been a professional in the software world, and then—for eight years—a stay-at-home mom. In May 2008, Skillsoft recruited her, generously allowing her to telecommute full-time from home. She loved being back at a fast-paced company and helping clients utilize Skillsoft's services. But three months into her new career, the banking crisis hit; businesses everywhere sputtered. In January 2009, the company reluctantly let her go. She left the corporate world and went back to school. Today she has her primary teaching credential and is thrilled to be substitute teaching; this fall, she will have her first permanent classroom.

I have received Ms. Fitzgerald's book proposal for *Canine Kitchen, Have Fun Making Easy and Nutritious Home-Cooked Meals for Your Dog*

Rebecca Fitzgerald, chef and dog lover, enjoyed feeding her animals the same nutritious food she cooked for her own table. Why not, she thought, create a canine cookbook and improve the lives of dogs everywhere? Her agent submitted the book to several small publishers; none bit.

My dear Senator

Wisconsin Senator Joseph McCarthy catapulted to the national stage in 1950 with a speech in which he claimed to know the names of more than two hundred Communists working for the State Department. He then sent a telegram to President Harry S Truman urging the commander in chief to expose them. It is unknown whether this stinging reply to McCarthy was ever delivered.

Dearest Scottie: I don't think I will be writing letters many more years

F. Scott Fitzgerald wrote this caustic letter to his daughter, Scottie, after her first year at Vassar College. He died two years later, the victim of a heart attack.

Steve—What happened to you?

She thought he just might be the one . . . until, she says, he cheated on her. Upon their breakup, Brandace sent Steve this scathing letter, expressing her disbelief and venting her fury. Brandace photocopied the letter before mailing it; now, four years later, whenever doubts creep in about ending the relationship, Brandace unfolds the letter and gives it a read.

At the moment I'm not up for the long drive thing

> **Date:** October 9, 2008 8:28:13 AM PDT
> **Subject:** RE: from eharmony
>
> Hey B,
>
> At the moment I'm not up for the long drive thing or should I say, more honestly, there are other eharmony opportunities that are a lot closer.
>
> H

After three months of online dating on eHarmony—which included five first dates, no second dates, and this kiss-off—Bess terminated her membership, vowing only to date men whom she'd met face-to-face. She is still single.

ACKNOWLEDGMENTS

At least four hundred people contributed to this book. But one stands out above all: chief reporter Betsy Towner Levine, who dug through archives, sweet-talked strangers, and led the letter collection team. I am grateful for her intelligence, diligence, and dedication. Theenks to the amazing Naomi Wax, who provided inspired ideas and unconditional encouragement. And to reporters Amy Bourne, Roslyn Schlenker, Mindy Griffiths, Rich Lord, Amy Chen, Jennifer Detweiler, Jennifer Hendriks, P. Davida Kales, Bethmarie Goulart Monson, Amy Kolczak, and Claire Vath.

Thanks to my wise agent, Brian Defiore, my brilliant editor, Doris Cooper, at Clarkson Potter, and to Lauren Shakely, Min Lee, Angelin Borsics, Amy Sly, and the entire Potter crew; to Maura Fritz and Matthew Snyder for their big ideas and generous ways.

And to all those who either (1) scraped through the past to share their own low moments or (2) coughed up evidence of when they made someone else feel like dirt: Bill Owens, Liz Arnold, Zoe Gayl, Lauren Decker, Meghan Staveler, Bill Dobrow, Barnaby Harris, Judy Harris, Jeff Harris (in absentia), John Natsoulas, Michael Hearst and One Ring Zero, Richard Barrett, Danny Green, Eva Spiegel, William Georgiades, Bones & The Electric Flea, Koni Stone, Corinne, Kelsey Fuller, the Smoking Gun at www.thesmokinggun.com, Michael Chabon, Tony Stamolis, Sarah Gray Miller, Margaret Evans, Stephanie Campisi, Alex Levine, Phoebe Levine, Molly McFadden, the fantastic blog Literary Rejections on Display (literaryrejectionsondisplay.blogspot.com), Adam Mansky, John Fox, Alex Dally MacFarlane, Lizzie LaRock, Chad Hardy, Stephanie Gibson, Matthew Martin, Peter Janssen, Michael D. Polensek, Elizabeth A. Spear, Peak Performance Health Club, Brian Shelley, Anya Strzemien, Blankee, Basha, Recycled Paper Greetings, Beth Wodzinski, Henry Goldblatt, Tom Stinson, Brenda C., the Athens Gang, Leyla Yildiz, Howard and Mary Fritz, Anna Jane Grossman, Rosellen Brown, PETA.org, Becky Kim, Al Rose, Jimi Geiyer, Olivia Combe, Harvey Wax, Mary Towner, Eileen Conlan, Chris Napolitano, Macuume, Sherry Mills, Clayton Anderson, Jacki Balderama, Howard Cooperstein, Derrick Bang, Sarah Lincoln, Julie Beer, Thea, Kevin Burg, Scott Pritchard, David Detweiler, Gretchen Hoffman, Amy Irvine, Holly Stewart, Melissa LaMunyon, Alex Bhattacharji, Brandace Laska, Colleen W. LeBlanc, Alex LeBlanc, Bobbie Lieberman, Steve Doten, Harry Gilonis, Lauren Wolfe, Michael Stutz, Greg Garry, Todd Linden, Patty Burke, Jim Lockwood-Stewart, Jorge Sanchez of www.jorgesanchez.org, Gary Winters, Mondonna Mostofi, Laura Smith-Black, Robert Riche, Matthew M. Scates, Haley Smernoff, ISPNR, Carrie Weinrich, Craig Gerard. And, of course, to my family: Sasha, Soren, Mom, Dad, Vicki, Dean, Haim, and Little Jacob.